Microwave Magic
Beef

Grolier Limited
TORONTO

Contributors to this series:

Recipes and Technical Assistance:
École de cuisine Bachand-Bissonnette
Cooking consultants:
Michèle Emond, Denis Bissonnette
Photos:
Laramée Morel Communications
Audio-Visuelles
Design:
Claudette Taillefer
Assistants: Joan Pothier
Julie Deslauriers
Philippe O'Connor
Accessories: Andrée Cournoyer
Editing: Communications
La Griffe Inc.

Assembly: Marc Vallières
Vital Lapalme
Carole Garon
Jean-Pierre Larose
Production Manager:
Gilles Chamberland
Art Director:
Bernard Lamy
Consultants:
Roger Aubin
Joseph R. De Varennes
Gaston Lavoie
Jocelyn Smyth
Donna Thomson
Production:
Le Groupe Polygone Éditeurs Inc.

The series editors have taken every care to ensure that the information given is accurate. However, no cookbook can guarantee the user successful results. The editors cannot accept any responsibility for the results obtained by following the recipes and recommendations given.

Canadian Cataloguing in Publication Data

Beef
(Microwave magic ; 1)
Translation of: Le Boeuf.
Includes index.
ISBN 0-7172-2375-2

1. Microwave cookery.   2. Cookery (Beef).
I. Series: Microwave magic (Toronto, Ont.) ; 1.

TX832.B8313 1987   641.5'882   C87-094417-7

Contents

Note from the Editor

How to Use this Book
The books in this set have been designed to make your job as easy as possible. As a result, most of the recipes are set out in a standard way.

We suggest that you begin by consulting the information chart for the recipe you have chosen. You will find there all the information you need to decide if you are able to make it: preparation time, cost per serving, level of difficulty, number of calories per serving and other relevant details. Thus, if you have only 30 minutes in which to prepare the evening meal, you will quickly be able to tell which recipe is possible and suits your schedule.

The list of ingredients is always clearly separated from the main text. When space allows, the ingredients are shown together in a photograph so that you can make sure you have them all without rereading the list—

another way of saving your valuable time. In addition, for the more complex recipes we have supplied photographs of the key stages involved either in preparation or serving.

All the dishes in this book have been cooked in a 700 watt microwave oven. If your oven has a different wattage, consult the conversion chart that appears on the following page for cooking times in different types of oven. We would like to emphasize that the cooking times given in the book are a minimum. If a dish does not seem to be cooked enough, you may return it to the oven for a few more minutes. Also, the cooking time can vary according to your ingredients: their water and fat content, thickness, shape and even where they come from. We have therefore left a blank space on each recipe page in which you can note

the cooking time that suits you best. This will enable you to add a personal touch to the recipes that we suggest and to reproduce your best results every time.

Although we have put all the technical information together at the front of this book, we have inserted a number of boxed entries called **MICROTIPS** throughout to explain particular techniques. They are brief and simple, and will help you obtain successful results in your cooking.

With the very first recipe you try, you will discover just how simple microwave cooking can be and how often it depends on techniques you already use for cooking with a conventional oven. If cooking is a pleasure for you, as it is for us, it will be all the more so with a microwave oven. Now let's get on with the food.

The Editor

Key to the Symbols
For ease of reference, the following symbols have been used on the recipe information charts.

The pencil symbol ✏️ is a reminder to write your cooking time in the space provided.

Level of Difficulty

🍴 Easy

🍴🍴 Moderate

🍴🍴🍴 Complex

Cost per Serving

$ Inexpensive

$ $ Moderate

$ $ $ Expensive

Power Levels

All the recipes in this book have been tested in a 700 watt oven. As there are many microwave ovens on the market with different power levels, and as the names of these levels vary from one manufacturer to another, we have decided to give power levels as a percentage. To adapt the power levels given here, consult the chart opposite and the instruction manual for your oven.

Generally speaking, if you have a 500 watt or 600 watt oven you should increase cooking times by about 30% over those given, depending on the actual length of time required. The shorter the original cooking time, the greater the percentage by which it must be lengthened. The 30% figure is only an average. Consult the chart for detailed information on this topic.

Power Levels

HIGH: 100% - 90%	Vegetables (except boiled potatoes and carrots) Soup Sauce Fruits Browning ground beef Browning dish Popcorn
MEDIUM HIGH: 80% - 70%	Rapid defrosting of precooked dishes Muffins Some cakes Hot dogs
MEDIUM: 60% - 50%	Cooking tender meat Cakes Fish Seafood Eggs Reheating Boiled potatoes and carrots
MEDIUM LOW: 40%	Cooking less tender meat Simmering Melting chocolate
DEFROST: 30% **LOW: 30% - 20%**	Defrosting Simmering Cooking less tender meat
WARM: 10%	Keeping food warm Allowing yeast dough to rise

Cooking Time Conversion Chart

700 watts	600 watts*
5 s	11 s
15 s	20 s
30 s	40 s
45 s	1 min
1 min	1 min 20 s
2 min	2 min 40 s
3 min	4 min
4 min	5 min 20 s
5 min	6 min 40 s
6 min	8 min
7 min	9 min 20 s
8 min	10 min 40 s
9 min	12 min
10 min	13 min 30 s
20 min	26 min 40 s
30 min	40 min
40 min	53 min 40 s
50 min	66 min 40 s
1 h	1 h 20 min

* There is very little difference in cooking times between 500 watt ovens and 600 watt ovens.

Beef: A Choice Meat

Of all the types of meat that human beings choose to eat, beef is the most popular. This is true even though its consumption is forbidden by religion in countries such as India, it is exorbitantly priced in Japan (you can pay up to $60 U.S. for a steak in a Tokyo restaurant), and it is not part of the cookery traditions of certain places (such as Hawaii).

It is true to say that, throughout Canada, beef is a major part of almost every menu and is eaten on a variety of occasions. Be it Sunday dinner with the family, a hasty bite at McDonald's or a gastronomic feast, it is most often beef that we choose to eat. This no doubt explains why there are more than a billion head of beef cattle in the world—enough to fill many plates. It also explains why we inherited so many ways of preparing this tasty red meat.

Cuts of Beef

Generally, the 25 cuts of beef sold in Canada are very similar to cuts sold in the United States, England and France, though they may have different names. Judging the quality of a cut of beef is almost an art in itself. You must consider fat content, color, texture and firmness. A classification system for beef is therefore a great help.

Whether you use a conventional cooker or a microwave oven, both the method of cooking and the cooking time vary according to the tenderness of the cut chosen. Most tender cuts can be cooked at high power levels for a relatively short period; less tender cuts require longer, slower cooking times at lower power levels. However, while the microwave oven gives the same results as the conventional cooker, it has the advantage of saving valuable time.

Beef is classified into three levels of tenderness: very tender, medium tender and less tender. Tender beef is cut from the upper central portion of a side of beef: rib, loin and sirloin. Medium tender beef is cut from the ends of the carcass, namely the hip and the chuck. Finally, the less tender beef cuts are those from the neck, brisket tip, shank, full brisket and the flank.

The type of cut is far from being the only factor that affects the quality and taste of beef, however. You must also take into account the fat content of the meat, the age of the animal, the firmness of the meat and its color. As most of us do not have any training in butchery, the Canadian government has instituted a classification system for beef that prides itself on being one of the best in the world.

The system sets out five general categories or grades. The meat that is most readily available, and the most popular, is from Canada A grade.

Canada A Grade

This grade is subdivided into four levels (A1, A2, A3 and A4) according to the amount of external fat. Canada A1 has the least fat, while Canada A2 and A3 have more external fat, and usually more marbling. Finally, Canada A4 cuts have the most fat and yield less actual meat, which affects the price. In Canada, 71% of the beef produced is Canada A.

Canada B Grade

This is lower quality beef that comes from young animals. Beef from this grade, which also has four subdivisions, is mainly supplied to institutions. This grade accounts for not quite 3% of the beef that is graded.

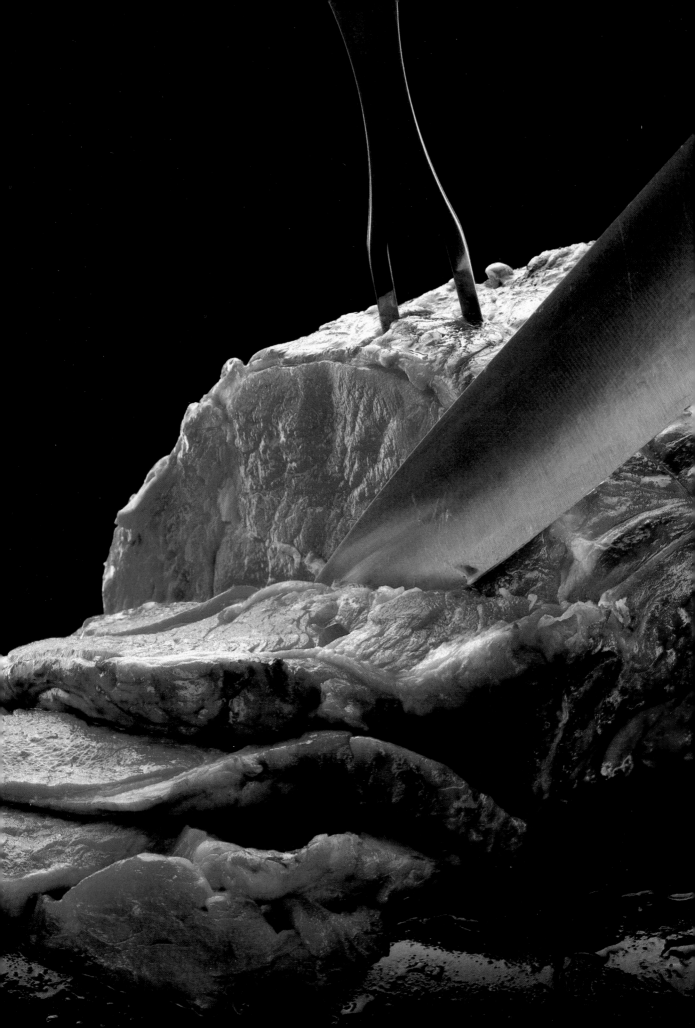

Canada C Grade

This category includes meat from intermediate-aged cattle and meat from young steers that does not meet the standards of the preceding categories. Meat of this grade is either used in meat products or sold to the meat trade. It represents just 4% of the beef produced in the country.

Canada D Grade

This category is for cuts from mature cows. Meat of this quality is generally used to make meat products and ground beef. It forms a relatively large part of overall beef production in Canada (21%).

Canada E Grade

Meat in this category comes from mature steers. It is used in similar ways to Canada D meat.

To make these grades more easily recognizable, federal government inspectors give meat a color-coded brand. Canada A beef is marked in red, B in blue and C in brown. Canada D and E are marked in black. The chart opposite summarizes all the information given above.

Cuts of Beef

Type of Cut	Cooking Method/ Power Level
Tender Cuts	
Rib roast	Roasting/ 70%
Steaks (rib, tenderloin, striploin, T-bone, sirloin)	Browning dish and roasting/ 100%
Medium Tender Cuts	
Sirloin tip roast, cross rib, rump, top round, eye of round	Roasting/ half of the cooking at 70% the other half at 25%
Cross rib, blade (chuck), outside round	Braising-stewing/ 70% or slower cooking at 25%
Less Tender Cuts	
Shoulder, brisket tip	Marinate and stew at 25%

Grades of Beef

Grade	Subdivision	Type of Animal	Comments
Canada A (red brand)	A1, A2, A3, A4	Young steers	Highest quality meat. Flesh is lean, bright red, with a firm texture. Light marbling. Fat is firm and white.
Canada B (blue brand)	B1, B2, B3, B4	Young animals	Flesh is lean, moderately dark, with moderately firm texture. No marbling. Fat varies from white to yellowish, and may be a bit soft.
Canada C (brown brand)		Young or intermediate-aged animals	Quality somewhat inferior to Canada A and B meat
Canada D (black brand)		Mature cows	
Canada E (black brand)		Mature steers	

Special Characteristics of Meat and Microwaving

Various characteristics of meat affect the way in which it should be cooked. The quantity and distribution of fat are the most important factors. Also to be taken into account are the amount of bone and its position in the meat, the size of the piece of meat and its shape. Finally, the choice of cooking method will depend on the tenderness of the cut.

1.
Meat that is well marbled with fat is generally more tender than very lean meat. The fine lines of fat in the meat give it an excellent texture, enhance the taste and help to retain the juices during cooking.

2.
To illustrate just how microwaves are distributed in the microwave oven we did a very simple test. We arranged slices of cheese on a plate

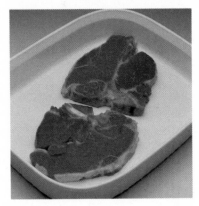

The shape of pieces of meat affects their cooking. For example, you should put a round, evenly shaped roast in the center of the cooking dish. Irregularly shaped pieces of meat should be arranged so that the thinner parts are towards the center of the dish.

The size of the pieces must also be taken into account. When preparing cubes of meat, it is preferable to cut them all to the same size, about 2.5 cm (1 inch). However, if the cubes are not of equal size, put the larger ones around the edges of the dish and the smaller ones towards the center.

To ensure even cooking, arrange meat that contains a bone with the bony parts facing inwards, where the microwaves are less intense.

11

and put them in the oven at 100% power. As you can see, the cheese around the edge of the plate cooked faster than the cheese in the center. These results demonstrate why food should be arranged with the thinner parts towards the inside in order to ensure even cooking. We recommend that you try the same test with your oven, because the distribution of energy can vary from one brand of oven to another.

3.
Meat is often covered with fat. If the layer of fat is of the same thickness throughout, the cooking will be more even. Conversely, if the layer of fat is not the same throughout, the meat that is close to thicker fat will tend to cook more quickly. We therefore recommend that you trim off excess fat in order to obtain more even cooking.

4.
Several cuts of beef include a bone, and you must take this into account when cooking the meat. For example, if the bone is less than 2.5 cm (1 inch) from the surface of the meat, it will reflect micro-waves onto the surrounding meat and so speed up the cooking of that part. On the other hand, bones that are in the center of a piece of meat and more than 2.5 cm away from the surface will have little effect on how long the meat takes to cook. We therefore recommend that pieces of meat containing a bone be arranged so that the bony parts are towards the inside.

5.
Not all pieces of beef have a nice even shape. Once again, irregularly shaped pieces should be arranged so that the thinner parts are towards the inside. It may also be beneficial to cover the thinner parts with aluminum foil, taking care to put the shiny side down, next to the meat.

6.
Because the ends of a piece of meat necessarily face outwards, they will tend to cook more quickly. To ensure even cooking, you should shield them from the microwaves by covering them with aluminum foil.

7.
The thickness and the size of pieces of meat also affect cooking time. This factor is particularly important for dishes such as stews that include several pieces of meat. If the cubes of beef are not of equal size, place the larger ones closer to the outside and the smaller ones closer to the center.

The Appearance of Meat: Browning

The most common criticism of microwave cooking concerns the appearance of meat. Many people say that roasts and other types of meat do not brown in the microwave process. These claims are quite unjustified.

After all, you sometimes have to brown a roast of pork, a chicken or some other types of meat before you put them in a

conventional oven in order to give them an attractive golden-brown appearance. You should be neither surprised nor discouraged to find it necessary to do the same before cooking meat in a microwave oven. All you have to do is heat a special dish called a browning dish in the oven at 100% power for about seven minutes. Then you add oil and put it back in the oven for 30

seconds. When you take it out of the oven, the oil is hot. You can then add the meat and brown it all over before beginning the actual cooking.

There are also special browning agents you can brush onto the surface of meat to give it a good color. Although the results are convincing, we do not recommend the use of these products because we think they mask the flavor of the meat. Decisions of this kind in cooking are, of course, a matter of taste. We have therefore drawn up a short list of browning agents currently used for beef so that you can try them and decide for yourself whether to use them or not.

Sauces and Seasonings for Browning

Soy sauce, Teriyaki sauce, barbecue sauce, brown and fruit sauces with melted butter added, Worcestershire sauce, steak sauces mixed with water, onion soup mix from a packet, liquid or powdered beef stock and spicy Mexican seasonings: any of these sauces and seasonings brushed over meat before cooking will help give it an attractive color and add flavor.

△   △

IN A MICROWAVE OVEN   *IN A CONVENTIONAL OVEN*

A reasonably fatty piece of meat cooked in a microwave oven for more than ten minutes will turn nicely brown. Larger pieces, such as a rib roast, will have the same pleasing appearance as those cooked in a conventional oven, but the surface will not dry out.

Browning Agents

Agent	Meat	Comments
Soy sauce or Teriyaki sauce	Beef patties, roasts	Apply with brush
Barbecue sauce	Beef patties, ribs	Apply with brush or pour over
Brown sauce and melted butter	Beef patties, roasts	Apply with brush
Worcestershire sauce	Beef patties, steaks, roasts	Apply with brush
Mix for onion soup or onion sauce, stock powder	Beef patties, roasts	Sprinkle over meat before putting in oven
Taco seasoning	Beef patties	Sprinkle over meat before putting in oven

14

Buying and Storing Beef

The quality of a cooked dish depends on the quality of the ingredients. You cannot expect to turn a rancid piece of meat into a juicy, tasty roast. To avoid disappointment, you must know not only how to choose beef but also the best way to store it.

Choose meat that has firm, creamy-white fat. Avoid meat in which the fat is yellow, soft or oily-looking. The flesh should be firm and lightly marbled with fat, and the bone, if there is one, should be porous and reddish in appearance. The meat should always have a bright color, whether it is light red or dark red. The chart on this page will help you decide how much meat to buy per serving depending on your choice of cut.

Recommended Quantities for Different Cuts

Cut	Amount per serving
Steaks and boneless roasts	115 g to 140 g (1/4 to 1/3 lb)
Rib roasts and braising cuts	140 g to 225 g (1/3 to 1/2 lb)
Round steak	140 g to 225 g (1/3 to 1/2 lb)
Cuts containing a lot of fat and bone (rump, short rib, shank)	450 g (1 lb)

How Much to Buy

When you buy meat, remember that the amount you need depends on more than the number of people who will be eating. You must take into account the appetite of different members of the family and of your guests, the way in which the meat will be served and the amount of fat and bone in the meat.

Choose roasts that weigh at least 1.5 kg (about 3 pounds). If this quantity is more than you need, plan one or more meals to use up the leftovers.

It is better to buy meat according to its cost per serving rather than its cost per kilogram. For example, a chuck roast with a bone yields two servings per 450 g (about 1 pound), while a boneless roast of the same weight yields three servings. So if the cost of a boneless cut is no more than 30% higher than that of the same cut with the bone, then the overall cost per serving is lower. The boneless meat becomes the better buy.

MICROTIPS

Freezing Irregularly Shaped Cuts

If you use aluminum foil to wrap irregularly shaped pieces of beef, we suggest that you wrap any protruding ends before you wrap the entire piece, so that these parts have the protection of the extra layer in the event of the outer wrapping being torn.

We recommend that you use vacuum-sealed freezer bags, which provide the best protection for your meat.

Freezing Beef

Beef, like other types of meat, keeps well in the freezer. This characteristic allows you to buy in quantity and to take advantage of the many special offers from your butcher or food store. However, freezing foodstuffs requires a certain amount of care and planning so as to avoid waste and loss of flavor.

Wrapping

The proper ways of storing meat all aim to prevent micro-organisms from breeding. In the past this was done by drying meat and salting it. Sailors, who often had to spend weeks without sighting land, would no doubt have a lot to say about the nature of meat stored and prepared in this manner.

Fortunately for us, there now exists a way of storing beef so that its original flavor remains intact. Nonetheless, while freezing is a simple method that everyone can use, the meat does require a certain amount of careful preparation before it is exposed to such low temperatures, because the cold, dry air can affect it and cause it to deteriorate. You must therefore protect

Vacuum-packing before freezing is the safest way to protect your expensive roasts and other meats from freezer burn.

meat by putting it in a wrapping that is airtight and watertight. Contact with the air would cause the meat to dry out and turn brown. This is known as freezer burn. You should also make sure that the wrapping does not allow liquids either in or out. If, for instance, blood or meat juices leaked out and got into a package of vegetables, not only would the meat be spoiled because of the loss of liquid but the flavor of the vegetables would also be affected and the vegetables might be ruined. Since many containers and dishes that cannot be used in a conventional oven can be used in a microwave, it is

possible for you to plan the freezing of your foodstuffs so that they can be put directly into the microwave for defrosting or cooking. You can use plastic bags and containers or even wrappings that can be vacuum-sealed. But, regardless of the wrapping or the container, you must always make sure that:

1. the package is hermetically sealed;

2. the contents, quantity, date on which it was put in the freezer and the maximum time it may be stored are clearly written on a label stuck to the package.

16

Roasts

Unless you have a device for vacuum-packing, we recommend that you wrap roasts in plastic wrap or aluminum foil, taking care to mold the wrapping tightly around the meat.

Steaks and Patties

In order to make a well-sealed package that fits easily into the freezer, we recommend that you stack steaks and patties. Put a piece of waxed or plastic-coated paper between each one so that they are easy to separate when you come to defrost them.

Cooked Dishes

In most cases, cooked dishes are frozen so that they can be put directly into the microwave oven for defrosting and reheating. To make this as easy as possible, put a freezer bag inside a plastic container. When you take it out of the freezer you simply put everything into the microwave.

Liver

To make defrosting easier, fold slices of liver before putting them in the freezer.

Storage Times for Meat

Cut	Refrigerator	Freezer
Roasts	3 days	8 to 12 months
Steaks	3 days	6 to 9 months
Stewing Beef	2 days	6 months
Ground Beef	2 days	3 to 6 months
Offal	1 to 2 days	3 months
Cooked Beef	7 days	3 months

Wrap the meat well in the appropriate wrapping, which should be airtight and watertight, to avoid freezer burn.

There are some very practical and easy-to-use freezer bags on the market. They provide a completely airtight seal. If you don't have this type of bag you can use ordinary bags and suck the air out of them with a straw.

An advantage of the microwave oven is that you can use the same dishes for freezing as for cooking. Plastic containers, in particular, can be ideal for both purposes. You don't have to buy extra dishes when you get your first microwave oven.

When fastening freezer bags that are to go directly into the microwave oven, don't use ties with a metal rib. Instead, use plastic ties designed specifically for the microwave oven.

MICROTIPS

For a TV Dinner in Just a Few Seconds

Whether you buy them ready made or make them yourself, TV dinners are just the thing for the microwave oven.

If the prepared dish has been frozen in its original commercial wrapping, usually a disposable aluminum plate, put it on a serving plate suitable for the microwave oven. Your meal will be ready in no time. However, if you prefer to prepare your own recipes, make them in the usual manner, divide them into three or four servings and put them on serving plates that can go in the freezer. Then, when you're really pressed for time, you can just take the plate from the freezer and put it in the oven.

You can eat really well even when you're on the run.

Defrosting

With proper freezing and careful defrosting, beef will retain all its original flavor. An advantage of the microwave oven is that it enables you to defrost your meat both quickly and carefully.

Defrosting Roasts

To be perfectly honest, defrosting is best done slowly in the refrigerator. However, life is so hectic these days that few of us have the time to wait. We must therefore make some compromises. When it comes to defrosting, a compromise is acceptable if it allows the food to defrost evenly so that the meat loses as little of its juices as possible during the process. In other words, it is not acceptable to let some parts of the meat start to cook while others are still frozen. Also, you should make sure that the meat does not come into contact with the juice that does seep out: liquids attract microwaves, and any parts of the meat left standing in them would begin to cook. There are three steps you can take to ensure good results:

1. Put an upside-down plate or saucer in a cooking dish and stand the meat on it. In this way the meat will not come into contact with the juice that accumulates in the dish.

2. After the first defrosting

Defrosting Guide

Cut	Defrosting Time at 50%	Defrosting Time at 25%
Rib, rump, eye of round, sirloin tip	12 to 14 min/kg (5-1/2 to 6-1/2 min/lb)	18 to 27 min/kg (9 to 13 min/lb)
Tenderloin, chuck roast, large steaks	7-1/2 to 9-1/2 min/kg (3-1/2 to 4-1/2 min/lb)	15 to 20 min/kg (7 to 9 min/lb)
Small steaks	6-1/2 to 9 min/kg (3 to 4 min/lb)	13 to 18 min/kg (6 to 8 min/lb)
Cubes of beef 2.5 cm (1 inch)	7 to 12 min/kg (3 to 5-1/2 min/lb)	12 to 22 min/kg (5 to 10 min/lb)
Ground beef	7-1/2 to 10 min/kg (3 to 5 min/lb)	12 to 15 min/kg (5 to 7-1/2 min/lb)

Don't forget to divide the defrosting time into two or three periods in the microwave with periods of standing time equal to a quarter of the total defrosting time in between.

cycle, touch the meat and cover any warm parts with aluminum foil (the thinner parts, the ends and the bony parts).

3. Divide the total time required for defrosting in the microwave into several short periods and allow a standing time equal to one-quarter of the total defrosting time in between.

Defrosting Ground Beef

There is no mystery about how to defrost ground beef in the microwave. You can in fact choose from three separate methods depending on the shape in which the meat was frozen. Freezing in a ring dish is the best way to obtain even defrosting. Since there is less microwave power in the center of the oven and, consequently, in the center of a dish, the ring shape is useful because there is no meat in the center.

Square Package

Place the wrapped package of frozen meat in the oven. Defrost it to the point where you can remove the meat from its container.

Place the meat in a microwave dish and set the oven for a second defrosting period.

At the end of the second defrosting period, scrape off any defrosted meat.

Put the rest of the meat in a dish and break it into pieces. Put it in the oven for a third and final defrosting period.

If there is more than 500 g (1 lb) of meat left at this stage, interrupt the defrosting to remove any defrosted meat.

Finally, let the meat stand for five to ten minutes until it is soft but still just a bit icy.

Ring Shape

A ring dish is ideal for freezing and for defrosting and cooking ground beef. The energy of the micro-waves is more concentrated towards the outside of the dish, and defrosting will therefore be more even because there is no meat in the center.

If you are planning to make a meat sauce or a ground beef casserole and you have frozen your ground beef in a microwave-safe dish, you can combine the processes of defrosting and precooking. This approach saves you valuable time and avoids your having to handle the meat.

Patties

To defrost patties made from ground beef, arrange them in a serving dish either two by two or four by four.

Halfway through the defrosting time, turn them and put them back in the oven.

Defrosting Irregularly Shaped Pieces

To ensure even defrosting, protect the ends and the thinner parts by covering them with aluminum foil, taking care to put the shiny side down, next to the meat.

Utensils for Defrosting

There are several types of utensils suitable for defrosting meat. It is generally recommended that you put pieces of meat in a grooved dish (roasting or bacon rack) in which the meat cannot come into contact with the juices that seep out of it. If you do not have such a dish, you can put the meat on an upside down saucer in a bigger dish that will collect the juices that seep out of the meat as it defrosts.

It is important to divide the defrosting time in the oven into two or three equal periods. This allows you not only to check on how the defrosting is going but also to ensure that the effect of the microwaves is being distributed evenly. The same is true for the standing time recommended between the defrosting periods.

When the defrosting process is over, allow about five minutes standing time.

Arranging Cubes of Meat and Meatballs

Whether you are defrosting or cooking, put the largest pieces around the edge of the dish. If the meatballs or cubes are all the same size, arrange them in a circle around the edge of the dish.

Defrosting Steaks and Flat Pieces of Meat

The same principles apply to these cuts as to roasts. The important thing once again is to ensure even defrosting.

As a first step, place the wrapped piece of meat in the oven. Defrost it until it can be removed from its container. Take it out of the oven and remove the wrapping. Cover any parts that are defrosted with aluminum foil, turn the meat over and put it back in the oven for the second defrosting period. When the time is up, let the meat stand for about five minutes.

The piece of meat is completely defrosted when you can pierce it with a fork.

MICROTIPS

Defrosting and Cooking Combined

To combine defrosting and cooking cycles, freeze the meat in a microwave-safe dish. When you are ready to prepare your recipe, don't set the oven at the 50% or 30% level recommended for defrosting, but rather at 70%. Allow four to five minutes for each 500 g (1 lb) serving. Break the meat into pieces and move those that are the most cooked towards the center of the dish to ensure even microwaving.

Put everything back in the oven at 70% for another four to five minutes. The meat will begin to cook. Take it out of the oven when it begins to brown and let it stand for two minutes.

When dealing with **small steaks,** first take off as much of the wrapping as possible. If the pieces of meat have been stacked for freezing, separate them by inserting a knife blade between each. Put the meat on a roasting rack or an upturned plate.

As soon as possible, remove the rest of the wrapping and turn the steaks over. Put the meat back in the oven for the second and last period of microwaving. Allow to stand for five minutes.

Cooking Times

Most people who are dealing with a microwave oven for the first time ask about cooking times. The speed of microwave cooking has been so much talked about that people are left with the impression that overcooking by three seconds will blacken the beautiful roast that the family is eagerly awaiting at the table.

However, there is no reason for microwave cooking to be such a source of anguish.

Quite the opposite. Just as with a conventional cooker, cooking times are related to the cut of meat, its weight and, of course, the power level at which it is cooked. The temperature of the meat at the time it is put into the oven must also be taken into account, as must the water and fat content of the meat. Fatty meat tends to cook more quickly because fats attract microwave energy.

Although cooking times are given for each of the recipes, the chart on page 23 will serve as a guide if you wish to adapt your own beef recipes designed for a conventional oven.

Testing for Doneness

Whether your piece of beef is cooked in a microwave or a conventional oven, you test for doneness in the same way.

You can base your testing either on the internal temperature of the meat or, particularly in the case of braising cuts, on the tenderness of the piece. To find out whether or not such a piece of meat is done, use a fork. Meat that is properly done can be broken apart easily with a fork. If the meat is not tender, let it cook a little longer.

You can also use a fork to judge the internal temperature of a roast. Simply insert the fork into the middle of the piece, take it out and touch it with your fingers. If blood trickles from the meat and the fork is warm, the roast is rare. If very little blood trickles out, the roast is medium.

For a more accurate measure, it is recommended that you use a temperature probe or a meat thermometer. Some microwave ovens allow you to program cooking times according to the internal temperature of the meat. When you put the roast in the oven, you insert the probe into the center of the piece and you set it for the internal temperature that corresponds to the degree of doneness you want. When the probe indicates that the meat has reached that temperature, the oven automatically switches off.

You can also use a meat

Cooking Times for Beef in the Microwave Oven

Cut	Power Level	Cooking Time
Roast beef Rib, boneless rib, sirloin tip		
Very rare	70%	10 to 12 min/kg (5 min/lb)
Rare	70%	13 to 14 min/kg (6 min/lb)
Medium	70%	15 to 17 min/kg (7 min/lb)
Well Done	70%	18 to 19 min/kg (8 min/lb)
Braising beef Chuck, rump (turn the meat after 1 h of cooking)	25%	50 to 60 min/kg (22 to 27 min/lb)

VERY RARE

RARE

MEDIUM

WELL DONE

thermometer. Never put a metal meat thermometer in a microwave oven, however. It could cause arcing (sparking) and damage the oven.

Make sure that a meat thermometer has been designed for use in a microwave oven before you use it in this way. (There are several models on the market.) If your thermometer cannot be used in a micro-wave oven, put it into the piece of meat after the minimum length of time suggested for cooking to the desired degree of doneness. If the thermometer reading shows that the required internal temperature has been reached, let the roast stand for about ten minutes before serving it. If the meat is not adequately done, allow it to cook a little longer.

Before serving, let the meat stand for about ten minutes. This allows the internal temperatures to even out and finishes off the cooking. As a general rule, the temperature will go up about 5°C (10°F) by serving time. The meat is then juicier and tastier. Consult the following chart to see how the degree of doneness relates to internal temperature.

Degree of Doneness and Internal Temperature

	When taken from oven	After standing
Very rare	40°C (100°F)	45°C (110°F)
Rare	45°C (110°F)	50°C (120°F)
Medium rare	50°C (120°F)	55°C (130°F)
Medium well done	55°C (130°F)	60°C (140°F)
Well done	60°C (140°F)	65°C (150°F)

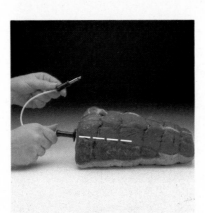

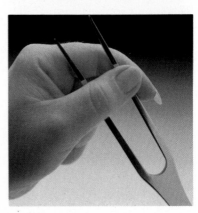

When allowing a piece of meat to stand after you bring it out of the oven, cover the dish (or, in the case of a roast, cover the meat directly) with aluminum foil placed shiny side down. This prevents the loss of heat which instead spreads evenly through the meat.

The temperature probe can be a very useful kitchen tool for cooking roasts and other pieces of meat. To get an accurate reading, take care to insert the end of the probe into the center of the meat. If the point is near a bone or too far from the center, the reading will be inaccurate and the results will not be as good.

If you don't have a temperature probe or a meat thermometer, you can still test for doneness. Simply push a carving fork into the center of the roast and leave it there for a few seconds. Take the fork out and touch it with your fingers. If it is very hot, the meat is well done, if it is warm, the roast is rare.

24

Chart for Cooking Beef

Practical Tips:

1. Always use a dish designed for microwave cooking.

2. After cooking, allow roasts to stand for about ten minutes before carving.

To check less tender cuts for doneness, pierce the meat with a fork. The meat is well done if the fibers break apart easily as you push the fork in.

MICROTIPS

Less tender cuts will literally melt in the mouth if they are allowed to soak in a cleverly seasoned marinade. Marinades loosen the fibers of the meat and allow the flavor of different seasonings to penetrate.

Food	Container	Cover	Power Level or Internal Temperature	
Ground beef	casserole	no	100%	1 kg : 8 to 13 min (1 lb : 4 to 6 min) (1-1/2 lb : 7 to 9 min)
Chunks of beef (for simmered dishes or soups)	casserole	yes	50%	1 kg : 45 min (1 lb : 20 min)
Meatballs	round plate or rectangular dish	waxed paper	100%	1 kg : 18 to 28 min (1 lb : 9 to 12 min) (1-1/2 lb : 10 to 13 min)
Meat loaf	round plate or deep rectangular dish	plastic wrap	100% 70% or 75% (170°F) internal temperature	Round loaf: 15 to 20 min Oblong loaf: 17 to 19 min
Braised roasts	rectangular dish or casserole	lid or plastic wrap	50%	43 to 55 min/kg (18 to 23 min/lb)
Stewed beef medium-tender cuts)	casserole	lid or plastic wrap	50%	1 kg : 45 min (1 lb : 20 min)
Tender roasts	rectangular dish with rack		70% very rare: 12 min/kg (5 min/lb) rare: 14 min/kg (6 min/lb) medium: 17 min/kg (7 min/lb) well done: 19 min/kg (8 min/lb) or using temperature probe: very rare: 40°C (100°F) rare: 45°C (110°F) medium rare: 50°C (120°F) well done: 60°C (140°F)	

Cooking Utensils

Practical Tips
1. Preheat the browning dish according to the manufacturer's instructions.
2. Do not salt the meat before cooking is complete.

Utensils and Dishes for Microwaves

If you have just obtained a microwave oven, do not rush out to the store to buy a complete set of dishes and utensils. Your kitchen cupboards are probably full of dishes that are perfectly suitable for microwave cooking. Any material that lets microwaves through can be used: glass, paper, pottery, porcelain (as long as it doesn't have a metallic trim), ceramic glass, straw or wicker baskets. As you can see, the list is long.

Browning dishes

There are dishes in which you can sear steaks, hamburgers, roasts, in short any meat the surface of which you want browned. A special coating, usually ferrite, applied to the bottom of these dishes absorbs microwaves and so gets very hot, which enables you to brown the meat.

IMPORTANT: Never use any metal dish or container in a microwave oven. It could cause sparking and damage the oven, and might even start a fire.

Shape of Containers

Allowing for the fact that only containers made of materials that let microwaves through can be used in a microwave oven, the shape of the container you choose has a direct bearing on the quality of the cooking.

Ring:
The microwaves penetrate the food from all sides. There is no food in the center, where cooking is slower.

Round:
The microwaves penetrate the food evenly from all sides, but since the center receives fewer microwaves food there cooks more slowly.

Square:
Food in the corners is doubly exposed to microwaves and runs the risk of being overcooked.

Guide to Cooking Utensils —

Rectangular:
Food in the corners is doubly exposed to microwaves and runs the risk of being overcooked. Food in the center cooks more slowly.

The choice of a suitable container is therefore very important. Note that the best ones are those that are shaped so as to allow equal exposure to the microwaves. But even if circular containers seem to be the most effective, other shapes can certainly be used. You will simply have to stir foods more frequently during cooking, turn them, cover them or reduce the power level.

	Usable
Aluminum foil	for protection
Dripping pan	no
Browning dish	yes
Brown paper bag	no

Tableware
    designated safe for use in a conventional
    oven and a microwave oven
	yes

Cardboard or polystyrene plate	yes

Glass or cup of
glass or ceramic
    heat resistant
    not heat resistant
	yes
	no

Metal container	no
Metal rack	no
Metal ties	no
Roasting bag	yes
Paper towel and paper serviettes	yes*
Microwave-safe plastic tableware	yes
Plastic wrap	yes

Thermometer
    designed for microwave oven
    designed for conventional oven
	yes
	no

Waxed paper	yes

* Never use paper containing synthetic fibers such as nylon, as these could cause a fire inside the oven.

MICROTIPS

Cooking Vegetables
Vegetables cooked in the microwave oven retain all their flavor and crispness.

Here are some tips that may be useful when cooking vegetables:
— for even cooking, choose vegetables that are the same size and shape;
— increase cooking time to match the quantity of vegetables being cooked at the same time;
— place the thinner parts of the vegetables towards the center of the oven, where the cooking is less intense;
— cover the dish during cooking and use a minimum amount of water;
— let the vegetables stand after cooking so that their texture is not spoiled;
— salt the vegetables after cooking them;
— to cook frozen vegetables in their wrapping, make a hole in the bag and place it on a piece of paper towel in the oven. Avoid cooking more than 225 g (8 oz) of vegetables at one time in this way, because they will not cook evenly.

Spices, Aromatics and Condiments for Beef

Good cooking is an art: it requires discernment and good taste. The master chef combines ingredients and seasonings with great skill in order to produce subtly flavored dishes that are virtually irresistible. The magic of spices is that they can transform the plainest fare into a gastronomic delight. But even though we have learned to appreciate the effect of spices, most of us know little about them. We will try here to give them the pride of place they deserve.

In practice, the term "aromatic" is applied to any substance used in the cooking process to enhance or add flavor, tenderize, make more acid, salty or oily. When these same substances are added at the table they are called condiments. An interesting point is that, with the exception of salt, all the substances used as aromatics or condiments come from plants.

Aromatics are classified according to their dominant flavor.

Sweet Aromatics: bay, juniper, rosemary, chervil, fennel, tarragon, basil, sage, parsley, aniseed, savory, mint, thyme, marjoram.

Pungent Aromatics: cumin, coriander, saffron, pepper, cinnamon, cloves, nutmeg.

As for condiments, they are classified in a more complex fashion.

Acid Condiments: vinegar, verjuice, lemon juice, etc.

Pungent Condiments: garlic, shallots, scallions, chives, onions, mustard, horseradish.

Pungent and Aromatic Condiments: lemon or orange zest, cocoa, coffee, pepper, paprika, sweet pepper, ginger.

Oily Condiments: oils, butter, fat.

Mixed Condiments: ready-made English sauces (such as Worcestershire sauce), ketchups, curry, blended mustards, soy sauce, etc.

We should emphasize that condiments are appetizing and aid digestion; however, using too much of certain pungent, salt or acid condiments can be harmful and cause stomach upsets.

Spices Used for Beef and Beef Sauces

Spice	Meat	Sauce
Bayleaves	Fricassee Braised beef	All marinades
Curry powder	All cuts	Marinades
Dill	All cuts	
Fines herbes	Roast liver Braised beef Stew Meat loaf Ground beef	
Ginger	Braising cuts Steak	Marinades
Marjoram	Braised beef	
Nutmeg	Meat loaf	
Oregano	Meat loaf	Spaghetti
Paprika	Ground beef	Barbecue
Rosemary	All cuts	Barbecue
Sage	Fricassee	
Seasoned salt	Steak Roasts	Barbecue Sauces for roasts
Thyme	Meat loaf Liver	Spanish

Rolled Sirloin Roast

Level of Difficulty	
Preparation Time	Roast: 10 min Sauce: 15 min
Cost per Serving	$ $
Number of Servings	6 to 8
Nutritional Value	6 servings: 356 calories 39.7 g protein 8.4 mg iron	8 servings: 267 calories 29.8 g protein 6.3 mg iron
Cooking Time	12 to 19 min/kg (5 to 8 min/lb)
Standing Time	10 min
Power Level	70%, 100%
Write Your Cooking Time Here	

Ingredients
1 sirloin roast
1 onion, sliced
50 mL (1/4 cup) mustard powder
pepper
50 mL (1/4 cup) butter

Garlic sauce:
2 cloves garlic, crushed
tea

Method
— Sprinkle the roast with pepper.
— Melt the butter at 100% for 30 seconds.
— Mix the mustard powder with the butter; brush it all over the roast.
— Tie the onion to the roast.
— Cook at 70% till done to your liking:

very rare:
   12 min/kg (5 min/lb)
rare:
   14 min/kg (6 min/lb)
medium:
   17 min/kg (7 min/lb)
well done:
   19 min/kg (8 min/lb)
or, using a temperature probe:
very rare: 40°C (100°F)
rare: 45°C (110°F)
medium rare:
   50°C (120°F)
medium well done:
   55°C (130°F)
well done: 60°C (140°F)
turning the meat one half-turn halfway through the cooking time.
— Deglaze, season and prepare a garlic sauce by adding two crushed cloves of garlic to the cooking juices.
— Add 125 mL (1/2 cup) strong tea per person.
— Heat through, scraping the bottom of the pan every minute.

N.B.: for a thicker sauce, add corn-starch mixed in a little cold water before the final cooking.

Mix the mustard with the butter you have melted in the microwave oven to obtain a uniform consistency.

Using a brush, coat the roast evenly with the butter-mustard mixture before cooking.

When the cooking is finished, cover the roast with aluminum foil and let it stand for 10 minutes before serving.

Cross Rib Roast

Level of Difficulty	 (icon)
Preparation Time	10 min
Cost per Serving	$
Number of Servings	4
Nutritional Value	381 calories 49 g protein 7.3 mg iron
Food Exchanges	5 oz meat 1 fat exchange
Cooking Time	14 to 22 min/ kg (6 to 9 min/lb)
Standing Time	10 min
Power Level	70%
Write Your Cooking Time Here	(pencil/apple icon)

Ingredients
1 roast 7.5 cm (3 inches)
thick, with a wide top surface
45 mL (3 tablespoons) butter
45 mL (3 tablespoons)
mustard
15 mL (1 tablespoon) soy
sauce
1 pinch basil

Method
— Combine the butter,
  mustard, soy sauce and
  basil.
— Brush the mixture over
  both sides of the roast.
— Cook on a rack at 70%
  till done to your liking:
  very rare:
    14 min/kg (6 min/lb)
  rare:
    17 min/kg (7 min/lb)
  medium:
    19 min/kg (8 min/lb)
  well done:
    22 min/kg (9 min/lb)
  or, using a temperature
  probe:
  very rare: 40°C (100°F)
  rare: 45°C (110°F)
  medium: 50°C (120°F)
  well done: 55°C (130°F)
  turning it halfway through
  the cooking time.
— Allow to stand for 10
  minutes and serve.

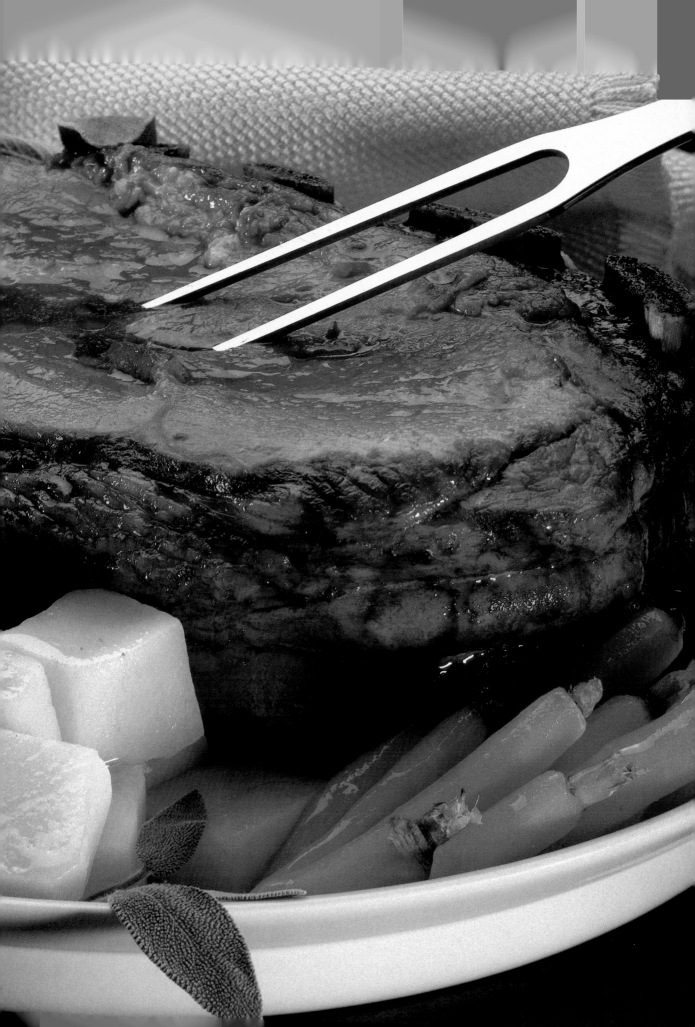

Bordelaise Sauce
Delicious with kebabs

Level of Difficulty	
Preparation Time	5 min
Cost per Serving	$
Number of Servings	4
Nutritional Value	79 calories
Food Exchanges	2 vegetable exchanges 1/2 fat exchange
Cooking Time	5 min
Standing Time	None
Power Level	100%
Write Your Cooking Time Here	

Ingredients
5 mL (1 teaspoon) butter
2 shallots
1 clove garlic
125 mL (1/2 cup) red wine
15 mL (1 tablespoon) parsley
250 mL (1 cup) hot stock
15 mL (1 tablespoon) soy sauce
15 mL (1 tablespoon) tomato paste
45 mL (3 tablespoons) cornstarch
60 mL (4 tablespoons) cold water
1 pinch thyme
1 pinch tarragon
salt and pepper

Method
— Mix together the shallots, garlic and butter; cook at 100% for 2 minutes.
— Mix the cornstarch with the cold water.
— Add all the other ingredients and cook at 100% for 2 minutes.
— Stir and continue cooking at 100% for 2 minutes.
— Stir again and continue cooking until the sauce thickens.

Béarnaise Sauce

An excellent accompaniment for steaks, green vegetables, poached eggs or fish

Level of Difficulty	🍴
Preparation Time	15 min
Cost per Serving	$
Number of Servings	4
Nutritional Value	260 calories
Food Exchanges	1 oz meat 4 fat exchanges
Cooking Time	2 min
Standing Time	None
Power Level	100%
Write Your Cooking Time Here	

Ingredients
4 egg yolks
10 mL (2 teaspoons) white vinegar
5 mL (1 teaspoon) tarragon
5 mL (1 teaspoon) dried onion flakes
2 mL (1/2 teaspoon) chervil
white pepper
125 mL (1/2 cup) butter
5 mL (1 teaspoon) fresh parsley

Method
— Put the egg yolks, vinegar, onions and spices in a mixer.
— Turn the mixer on to high speed and add the butter gradually through the opening in the cover; mix until the sauce thickens.
— Add the parsley. Serve hot.

MICROTIPS

Deglazing is done to make use of the juices that seep out from the meat during cooking.

To deglaze, pour a liquid (water, vinegar or a good dry wine) into the bottom of the dish in which the meat was cooked, and then add seasonings.

Scrape with a wooden spoon to remove solid particles and mix well. Heat and pour over the cooked meat before serving.

35

Ribs with Barbecue Sauce

Level of Difficulty	🍴
Preparation Time	20 min*
Cost per Serving	$
Number of Servings	3
Nutritional Value	408 calories 33 g protein 4.6 mg iron
Food Exchanges	4 oz meat 2 vegetable exchanges 1 fat exchange
Cooking Time	65 min
Standing Time	None
Power Level	100%, 50%
Write Your Cooking Time Here	

* The meat should be marinated for at least 24 hours.

Ingredients
900 g (2 lb) beef ribs
125 mL (1/2 cup) ketchup or chili sauce
250 mL (1 cup) water
15 mL (1 tablespoon) sugar
15 mL (1 tablespoon) prepared mustard
5 mL (1 teaspoon) salt
20 peppercorns
1 pinch savory
4 cloves garlic, cut in two
2 onions, thinly sliced
45 mL (3 tablespoons) soy sauce

Method
— Combine all ingredients other than the meat and mix well; add ribs.
— Allow to marinate for 24 hours in the refrigerator, stirring 2 or 3 times.
— Remove the ribs and boil the marinade at 100% for 5 minutes.
— Put the ribs back in and cook at 50% for 30 minutes.
— Stir the ribs and continue cooking at 50% for 30 minutes or until the meat is tender.

Assemble all the ingredients for the marinade and mix them together. The marinade will help to tenderize the meat and give it a pleasant flavor.

Put the beef ribs in the marinade and leave for 24 hours, stirring 2 or 3 times.

When the marinating is complete, remove the ribs before boiling the marinade.

MICROTIPS

Never preheat the browning dish for longer than the time specified in the recipe, or you might damage the inside wall of the oven.

Chuck Roast

Level of Difficulty	(icon)
Preparation Time	10 min
Cost per Serving	$
Number of Servings	6
Nutritional Value	310 calories 40.8 g protein 7.2 mg iron
Food Exchanges	4 oz meat 2 vegetable exchanges 1 fat exchange
Cooking Time	1 h 40 min
Standing Time	10 min
Power Level	100%, 50%
Write Your Cooking Time Here	(icon)

Ingredients
1.1 kg (2-1/2 lb) chuck roast
500 g (1 lb) whole green beans
salt and pepper
15 mL (1 tablespoon) oil
1 284 mL (10 oz) can beef consommé
750 mL (3 cups) hot water
60 mL (4 tablespoons) dried onion
30 mL (2 tablespoons) cornstarch

Method
— Preheat a browning dish at 100% for 7 minutes.
— Add oil and heat for 30 seconds.
— Sear the roast and place it in a casserole.
— Season; add green beans, liquid ingredients and dried onion.
— Cook at 100% for 10 minutes; reduce power level to 50% and continue to cook for 90 minutes or until the meat is tender. Turn meat over halfway through the cooking time.
— Remove meat and vegetables.
— Mix cornstarch with 15 mL (3 teaspoons) cold water; stir into the sauce and cook at 100% until thickened, stirring every 2 minutes.
— Add salt and pepper, and serve.

Preheat a browning dish at 100% for 7 minutes.

Pour oil into the preheated dish and put back in the oven for 30 seconds.

Put the roast in the dish and sear one side then the other in the hot oil.

When you have seared the roast, put it in a casserole. Add spices, green beans and all the other ingredients except the cornstarch.

Beef Stroganoff

Level of Difficulty	🍴🍴
Preparation Time	20 min
Cost per Serving	$
Number of Servings	6
Nutritional Value	334 calories 38.5 g protein 6.4 mg iron
Food Exchanges	5 oz meat 2 vegetable exchanges 1 fat exchange
Cooking Time	1 h
Standing Time	None
Power Level	100%, 50%
Write Your Cooking Time Here	

Ingredients

900 g (2 lb) beef, cut into strips
450 g (1 lb) mushrooms, sliced
1 onion, thinly sliced
30 mL (2 tablespoons) butter
30 mL (2 tablespoons) all-purpose flour
550 mL (2-1/4 cups) hot beef stock
salt
90 mL (6 tablespoons) tomato paste
10 mL (2 teaspoons) Worcestershire sauce
125 mL (1/2 cup) sour cream
chopped parsley

Method

— Combine mushrooms, onion and butter in a bowl; cover and cook at 100% for 5-1/2 to 6 minutes.
— Coat the beef with flour and sear it in a browning dish; combine browned beef and vegetables.
— Mix in stock, salt, tomato paste and Worcestershire sauce. Cover and cook at 100% for 5 minutes; stir.
— Reduce the power level to 50% and continue cooking for 45 minutes or until the meat is tender. Stir halfway through the cooking time.
— Add the sour cream and mix; garnish the top of the dish with parsley.

Assemble all the ingredients required to make the dish, then combine mushrooms, onion and butter in a bowl.

When you have floured and seared the strips of beef, mix them in with the vegetables.

Add the beef stock, salt, tomato paste and the Worcestershire sauce, and mix everything together well before starting the cooking.

When the cooking is finished, add the sour cream and mix well; sprinkle the dish with parsley and serve.

Steak Sukiyaki

	Single Recipe	Double Recipe
Level of Difficulty	🍴	🍴
Preparation Time	20 min	25 min
Cost per Serving	$ $ $	$ $ $
Number of Servings	3 to 4	6
Nutritional Value	322 calories 30.2 g protein 5.0 mg iron	
Food Exchanges	3 oz meat 2 vegetable exchanges 1 fat exchange	
Cooking Time	20 min	22 min
Standing Time	10 min	10 min
Power Level	100%, 50%	100%, 50%
Write Your Cooking Time Here		

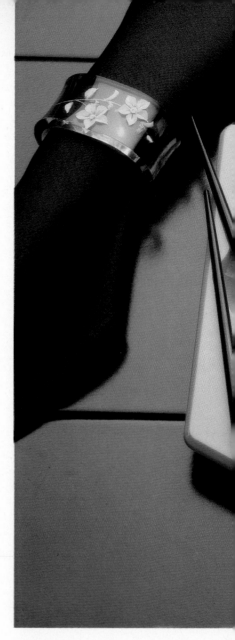

Ingredients

Single Recipe		Double Recipe
450 g (1 lb)	top round	900 g (2 lb)
225 mL (8 oz)	bamboo shoots	450 mL (16 oz)
50 mL (1/4 cup)	water chestnuts	125 mL (1/2 cup)
225 g (8 oz)	bean sprouts	450 g (16 oz)
5	green onions	8
225 g (8 oz)	mushrooms	450 g (16 oz)
3	celery stalks	6
30 mL (2 tablespoons)	oil	45 mL (3 tablespoons)
75 mL (1/3 cup)	soy sauce	125 mL (1/2 cup)
30 mL (2 tablespoons)	brown sugar	45 mL (3 tablespoons)
5 mL (1 teaspoon)	ground ginger	10 mL (2 teaspoons)
125 mL (1/2 cup)	beef consommé	250 mL (1 cup)

Method
— Drain then thinly slice bamboo shoots and water chestnuts.
— Bias-cut the green onions and celery; thinly slice the mushrooms and the meat.
— Preheat a browning dish at 100% for 7 minutes.
— Add 15 mL (1 tablespoon) oil and heat at 100% for 30 seconds.
— Sear the meat and add the vegetables.
— Heat the beef consommé, soy sauce, brown sugar and ground ginger at 100% for 2 minutes (4

minutes for the double recipe).
— Add the sauce to the other ingredients.
— Cover. Cook at 50% for 10 to 12 minutes. Stir halfway through the cooking time.
— Allow to stand, covered, for 10 minutes. Serve.

Like many dishes that come to us from the Orient, Steak Sukiyaki calls for meat and vegetables to be very thinly sliced.

MICROTIPS

Mushrooms
Store mushrooms in the refrigerator to keep them fresh as long as possible. Never soak mushrooms in water. To clean, you need only brush them.

Steak Sukiyaki

Place the meat in the center of the browning dish and arrange the vegetables around it.

Combine the beef consommé, soy sauce, brown sugar and ground ginger; heat the mixture.

Add the resulting hot sauce to the meat and vegetables. Cover and cook according to the recipe.

MICROTIPS

Steak Sukiyaki

How to Cook Using the Temperature Probe
The probe guarantees precise cooking for nearly all foods. Its use is based on a very simple principle: you insert it in the food to be cooked and choose the internal temperature that the food is to reach. When that temperature is reached, the oven automatically switches off. Instead of setting the oven for a certain number of minutes, you set the probe to the precise temperature required for a particular degree of doneness; you still have to set the power level. For good results, the probe must be inserted very carefully. In the case of meats, you must insert it so that its point is at the center of the thickest part, taking care to ensure that it is not touching bone or fat because these cook more quickly than the meat. Also we recommend that the probe be parallel to the plate.

Setting the Temperature Probe
40°C (100°F): Very rare beef
45°C (110°F): Rare beef
55°C (130°F): Medium beef
60°C (140°F): Fish steaks or fillets, well done beef
65°C (150°F): Fully cooked ham
68°C (155°F): Veal
71°C (160°F): Well done pork
74°C (165°F): Well done lamb
77°C (170°F): Chicken pieces (and other poultry)
82°C (180°F): Whole birds, well done

Macédoine of Beef

A special treat for vegetable lovers

Ingredients
700 g (1-1/2 lb) ground beef
salt and pepper
1 large green pepper, cut into
strips
3 carrots, thinly sliced
1 Spanish onion, thinly sliced
3 large potatoes, thinly sliced
2 284 mL (10 oz) cans
tomato soup
parsley
basil

Method
— Place the beef, onion,
green pepper, carrots,
potatoes, parsley and basil
in a rectangular dish; pour
in the tomato soup and
season.
— Cover and cook at 100%
for 20 minutes; turn halfway through the cooking
time.
— Allow to stand for 5
minutes and serve.

Level of Difficulty	🍴	
Preparation Time	30 min	
Cost per Serving	**$**	
Number of Servings	4 to 6	
Nutritional Value	4 servings: 649 calories 53.2 g protein 8.4 mg iron	6 servings: 433 calories 35.4 g protein 5.6 mg iron
Food Exchanges	4 servings: 5 oz meat 2 bread exchanges 3 vegetable exchanges 1 fat exchange	6 servings: 3 oz meat 1 bread exchange 2 vegetable exchanges 1 fat exchange
Cooking Time	20 min	
Standing Time	5 min	
Power Level	100%	
Write Your Cooking Time Here	✏️🍎	

To Tenderize Less Tender Cuts

Certain cuts of beef are less tender but more economical to buy. Marinating will tenderize them and, at the same time, give them an interesting flavor. Ribs with Barbecue Sauce, Beef Kebabs, Chinese Beef, and Beef Liver are all simple and easy-to-prepare recipes that rely on steeping the meat in a marinade for a certain length of time (which varies according to the recipe) before cooking it. As a result of the lengthy steeping in the liquid, the meat fibers become more tender and take on the flavor of the marinade.

Economical cuts such as cross rib, chuck, short ribs and flank are suitable for marinating, as are medium tender cuts such as round, rump and sirloin tip.

A marinade is quite simply a mixture of liquids and seasonings that can be put together in a few minutes from ingredients you have on hand in the kitchen. Be sure to pierce the meat with a long fork or to make incisions in steaks in order to let the marinade penetrate and take full effect. You must have enough liquid to cover the meat.

Beef Roulades with Mustard

Level of Difficulty	🍴🍴
Preparation Time	30 min
Cost per Serving	$ $ $
Number of Servings	6
Nutritional Value	478 calories 27.1 g protein 4.4 mg iron
Food Exchanges	4 oz meat 1 vegetable exchange 3 fat exchanges
Cooking Time	24 min
Standing Time	5 min
Power Level	100%, 70%
Write Your Cooking Time Here	

Ingredients

600 g (1-1/4 lb) beef tenderloin
2 large dill pickles
pepper
60 mL (4 tablespoons) Dijon mustard
8 slices bacon
1 onion, chopped
30 mL (2 tablespoons) butter
500 mL (2 cups) hot beef stock
15 mL (1 tablespoon) soy sauce
125 mL (1/2 cup) 35% cream
60 mL (4 tablespoons) cornstarch

Method

— Cut the meat into 8 thin slices and the pickles into 8 strips.
— Pepper each slice of beef and brush with mustard.
— Cook the chopped onion at 100% for 1 minute.
— Cook the bacon at 100% for 5 minutes.
— Place a slice of bacon on each slice of beef; sprinkle with cooked onion and top with a strip of pickle.
— Roll up the slices of beef carefully and secure each roll with a toothpick.
— Preheat a browning dish at 100% for 7 minutes; add butter and sear the meat on all sides.
— Pour the hot beef stock and the soy sauce over the meat.
— Cover and cook at 70% for 3 minutes; turn the roulades over and continue cooking for 2 minutes.
— Take the roulades out and set aside.
— Mix the cream with the cornstarch; stir into the sauce; whip the sauce and cook it for 6 minutes, stirring every 2 minutes.
— Put the roulades back in the sauce and reheat at

70% for 2 minutes.
— Allow to stand for 5
  minutes.
— Decorate with strips of
  pickle.
— Serve on a bed of noodles.

*The dill pickles, Dijon mustard
and bacon combine with the
other ingredients to give this
dish a distinctive taste.*

MICROTIPS

**To Separate Frozen
Bacon Slices**
Just heat the packet at
100% for 20 to 30
seconds. Gradually
remove defrosted slices.

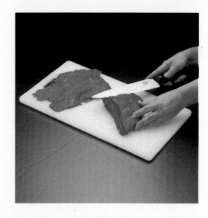

Cut the beef tenderloin into 8 thin slices and the pickles into 8 strips.

Brush each slice of meat with mustard, top with a slice of bacon and a strip of pickle, then roll and secure with a toothpick.

Pour the hot beef stock and the soy sauce over the roulades once you have seared them in a browning dish.

To thicken the sauce, stir in the cream and cornstarch mixture. Beat vigorously.

Put the roulades back in the sauce before finishing the cooking.

Decorate with strips of pickle and serve on a bed of noodles.

To Dry Herbs

Fresh herbs, such as basil, thyme or parsley, will normally keep only a few days in the refrigerator. With a microwave oven, however, drying herbs is simplicity itself.

First, wash the herbs while they are still fresh. Sponge them gently with paper towel, then leave them to finish drying for a few hours in the open air at room temperature. When there is no trace of moisture left, arrange 5 well-leaved sprigs of your herb in a circle on a glass plate lined with three sheets of paper towel. Cover with another sheet of paper towel and heat in the microwave at 100% for 1 minute. If the herbs are not dry enough, give the plate a half-turn and repeat. (Note that if herbs are over-heated they may burst into flames.)

Once the herbs have cooled, crumble the leaves and stems separately and store in an airtight container.

Filet Mignon

Considered by many to be the finest of all beef cuts,
filet mignon is sure to please your guests.

Level of Difficulty	🍴
Preparation Time	5 min
Cost per Serving	$ $ $
Number of Servings	4
Nutritional Value	377 calories 36.1 g protein 6.1 mg iron
Food Exchanges	8 oz meat
Cooking Time	3 min each
Standing Time	None
Power Level	70%
Write Your Cooking Time Here	

Ingredients
4 filet mignon steaks, each
weighing 225 g (1/2 lb)
60 mL (4 tablespoons) melted
butter
60 mL (4 tablespoons) soy
sauce

Method
— Mix the melted butter with
  the soy sauce.
— Brush the steaks with the
  sauce and put them on a
  rack.
— Cook each steak
  separately at 70% for
  1-1/2 minutes; turn over
  and continue cooking for
  1-1/2 minutes or until
  done to your liking.
— Repeat this step for each
  of the steaks.

Chinese Beef

Level of Difficulty	🍴🍴
Preparation Time	30 min*
Cost per Serving	💲 💲
Number of Servings	4
Nutritional Value	283 calories 24.7 g protein 3.9 mg iron
Food Exchanges	3 oz meat 1 vegetable exchange 1 fat exchange
Cooking Time	10 min
Standing Time	5 min
Power Level	100%
Write Your Cooking Time Here	

* The meat should be marinated for at least 1 hour.

Ingredients

450 g (1 lb) tender beef steak
45 mL (3 tablespoons) soy sauce
30 mL (2 tablespoons) sake or kirsch
5 mL (1 teaspoon) cornstarch
30 mL (2 tablespoons) vegetable oil
2 mL (1/2 teaspoon) salt
1 onion, thinly sliced
1 green pepper, thinly sliced
1 stalk celery, thinly sliced
4 small pieces fresh ginger root
4 green onions, finely chopped

Method

— Cut the meat diagonally into thin strips.
— Mix the meat with the soy sauce, sake or kirsch and the cornstarch. Allow to stand for 1 hour.
— Put the oil, salt, onion, green pepper and celery in a microwave-safe dish; cover and cook at 100% for 2 minutes; add the ginger root, cover again and continue cooking for 5 more minutes.
— Add the meat and sauce; stir well and spread evenly over the surface of the dish.
— Cook at 100% for 3 minutes; stir halfway through the cooking time and at the end.
— Garnish with the green onions and allow to stand, covered, for 5 minutes.

Onion, green pepper and celery are vegetables that are frequently used in oriental-style recipes.

52

Mix the meat with the soy sauce, sake or kirsch and the cornstarch, then allow to marinate for 1 hour.

While the meat is marinating, cut the onion, green pepper and celery and put them in a micro-wave-safe bowl.

When the cooking is finished, garnish with green onions, cover and allow to stand for 5 minutes before serving.

Beef with Celery and Bacon

Level of Difficulty	
Preparation Time	25 min
Cost per Serving	$
Number of Servings	4
Nutritional Value	492 calories 32.4 g protein 5 mg iron
Food Exchanges	4-1/2 oz meat 1 vegetable exchange 3 fat exchanges
Cooking Time	50 min
Standing Time	None
Power Level	100%, 50%
Write Your Cooking Time Here	

Ingredients
675 g (1-1/2 lb) beef, cubed
4 stalks celery
30 to 45 mL (2 to 3 table-spoons) oil
8 slices bacon, cut into strips
2 medium onions, thinly sliced
1 clove garlic, chopped
50 mL (1/4 cup) all-purpose flour
125 mL (1/2 cup) red wine
1 bouquet garni
300 mL (1-1/4 cup) beef stock
salt and pepper

Method
— Wash the sticks of celery and remove the strings; cut into thin strips.
— Brown the bacon at 100% for 4 minutes on the grill; drain.
— Heat a browning dish at 100% for 7 minutes; pour in the oil and heat again for 15 seconds.
— Cook the celery, onion and garlic in the browning dish; sprinkle with flour and add the wine a little at a time. Mix.
— Add the beef, bacon, bouquet garni and beef stock.
— Add salt and pepper; stir.
— Cover and cook at 100% for 5 minutes, then at 50% for 30 minutes.
— Before serving, adjust the seasoning, remove the bouquet garni and turn into a deep dish.

MICROTIPS

To Rid the Oven of Cooking Smells:
Mix a cup of water with the rind and juice of a lemon in a small glass bowl. Heat the mixture in the oven at 100% for 3 minutes. Wipe the inside of the oven with a damp cloth.

A Different Way to Serve Leftovers
You can reheat leftover beef to make delicious sandwiches. Simply put a few thin slices of meat inside a buttered bun. Heat for 1 minute at 50%.

A Simple Way to Make Garlic Butter
Melt 225 g (1 cup) butter or margarine with 3 cloves of garlic that you have peeled and cut in two. Allow to stand for 18 minutes and remove the garlic.

Beef Bourguignon

Level of Difficulty	🍴
Preparation Time	30 min
Cost per Serving	$ $ $
Number of Servings	8
Nutritional Value	314 calories 27.4 g protein 4.2 mg iron
Food Exchanges	3 oz meat 2 vegetable exchanges 1 fat exchange
Cooking Time	1 h 15 min
Standing Time	10 min
Power Level	100%, 50%
Write Your Cooking Time Here	

Ingredients
1.1 kg (2-1/2 lb) beef round, cubed
50 mL (1/4 cup) flour
5 mL (1 teaspoon) salt
8 peppercorns
50 mL (1/4 cup) oil
125 mL (1/2 cup) sliced leeks
125 mL (1/2 cup) sliced onions
125 mL (1/2 cup) thinly sliced carrots
1 clove garlic, thinly sliced
30 mL (2 tablespoons) parsley
30 mL (2 tablespoons) cognac
2 cloves
1 mL (1/4 teaspoon) marjoram
paprika
375 mL (1/2 bottle) red wine

Method
— Combine flour, salt and pepper in a cup.
— Preheat a roasting dish at 100% for 7 minutes; add the oil and brown the cubes of beef.
— Flour the browned beef; mix well. If possible, transfer the ingredients to a heavy casserole.
— Add the vegetables and the wine. Cover and cook at 100% for 4 to 5 minutes or until the liquid has come to a full boil.
— Heat the cognac, ignite and pour over the meat. Season; mix well.
— Cover. Cook at 50% for 60 to 70 minutes, or until the meat is tender. Stir halfway through the cooking time.
— Allow to stand for 10 minutes without removing the cover. Serve.

Cubes of beef round are ideal for this simple but tasty recipe.

Use a small sieve to sprinkle the cubes of browned beef evenly with flour before mixing well.

Add the wine immediately after the vegetables and bring to a boil before igniting the cognac and pouring it over the meat.

Beef in Beer

Level of Difficulty	🍴
Preparation Time	15 min
Cost per Serving	$
Number of Servings	6
Nutritional Value	342 calories 33.5 g protein 5.1 mg iron
Food Exchanges	4 oz meat 1/2 vegetable exchange 1 fat exchange
Cooking Time	1 h 15 min
Standing Time	10 min
Power Level	100%, 50%
Write Your Cooking Time Here	

Ingredients
1.1 kg (2-1/2 lb) beef, cubed
paprika
pepper
50 mL (1/4 cup) oil
250 mL (1 cup) sliced onions
45 mL (3 tablespoons) flour
15 mL (1 tablespoon) brown sugar
250 mL (1 cup) beer
125 mL (1/2 cup) beef consommé

Method
— Sprinkle the meat with pepper and paprika.
— Preheat a browning dish at 100% for 7 minutes; add the oil.
— Brown the cubes of beef and remove them.
— Add all the other ingredients; bring to a boil at 100%.
— Add the meat and cover. Cook at 50% for about an hour, or until the meat is tender. Stir halfway through the cooking time.
— Allow to stand for 10 minutes with the cover on. Serve.

A simple dish, calling for economical ingredients that are easy to obtain.

Place the cubes in a preheated browning dish containing oil and brown them evenly.

Add the browned meat to the mixture of onion, flour, brown sugar, beer and beef consommé once it has come to a boil.

MICROTIPS

To Peel Garlic Cloves More Easily
There is a very simple trick: just rinse them in hot water before peeling them.

Beef Kebabs

Level of Difficulty	🍴
Preparation Time	15 min*
Cost per Serving	$ $
Number of Servings	4
Nutritional Value	243 calories 25.1 g protein 3.9 mg iron
Food Exchanges	3 oz meat
Cooking Time	5 min
Standing Time	2 min
Power Level	70%
Write Your Cooking Time Here	✏️🍎

* The meat should be marinated for at least 1 hour.

Ingredients
16 cubes sirloin
2 mL (1/2 teaspoon) chili powder
2 cloves garlic, crushed
5 mL (1 teaspoon) ground cumin
5 mL (1 teaspoon) sugar
30 mL (2 tablespoons) soy sauce
1 onion, grated
15 mL (1 tablespoon) lemon juice
Vegetables of your choice

Method
— Combine all the ingredients except the beef cubes and vegetables.
— Add the meat to the mixture; allow to marinate for 1 hour.
— Skewer the cubes of beef on 4 wooden skewers, alternating with vegetables of your choice.
— Put the kebabs in a 20 cm (8 inch) square dish.
— Cook at 70% for 5 minutes if you want the meat cooked medium; cook a little longer for well done meat. Stop the cooking twice to give the dish a half-turn.
— Allow to stand for 2 minutes and serve.

Prepare the marinade by combining all ingredients except the beef and vegetables.

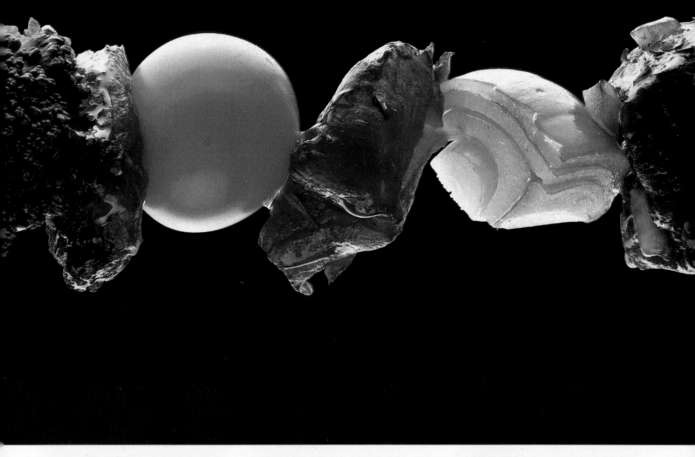

Add the meat to the marinade and allow to stand for 1 hour to tenderize the meat and give it a pleasant flavor.

When the meat is fully marinated, alternate cubes on 4 wooden skewers with vegetables of your choice and put them in a square dish.

Place the dish on a turntable in the microwave oven so you can give it a half-turn twice during the cooking process.

Vegetable Stew

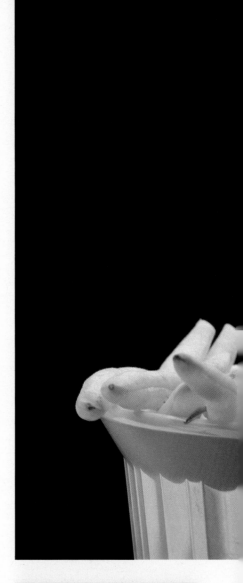

Level of Difficulty	🍴
Preparation Time	30 min
Cost per Serving	$ $
Number of Servings	6
Nutritional Value	331 calories 37.5 g protein 6.4 mg iron
Food Exchanges	2 oz meat 2 vegetable exchanges 1 fat exchange
Cooking Time	1 h 10 min
Standing Time	15 min
Power Level	100%, 50%
Write Your Cooking Time Here	

Ingredients
900 g (2 lb) top round, cubed
6 medium potatoes, diced
4 large carrots, cut into rounds
1 medium turnip, diced
3 small onions
225 g (1/2 lb) green beans
1.5 L (6 cups) water
15 mL (1 tablespoon) beef stock concentrate (Bovril)
salt and pepper
5 mL (1 teaspoon) tarragon
5 mL (1 teaspoon) parsley

Method
— Cook all the vegetables with a little water in a covered dish at 100% for 5 to 6 minutes.
— Mix the cooked vegetables in a 5 L container; add the water and beef stock concentrate; heat at 100% for 5 minutes.
— Add the meat and spices, cover and cook at 50% for 60 minutes or until meat is tender. Stir halfway through the cooking time.
— Allow to stand for 15 minutes and serve.

The large number of vegetables used in this traditional dish make it very nutritious.

Cut up the vegetables and put them in a microwave-safe casserole with a little water.

Precook the vegetables, then transfer them to a 5 L casserole and add the beef stock concentrate and the water.

Add the cubes of meat and the spices, cover and cook for 50 to 60 minutes or until the meat is tender.

T-Bone Steak

Level of Difficulty	🍴
Preparation Time	Minimal
Cost per Serving	$ $ $
Number of Servings	1
Nutritional Value	322 calories 48.75 g protein 7.25 mg iron
Cooking Time	4 min
Standing Time	None
Power Level	70%
Write Your Cooking Time Here	

Ingredients

1 T-bone steak weighing 225 g (8 oz)
5 mL (1 teaspoon) butter
5 mL (1 teaspoon) beef stock concentrate (Bovril)

Method

— Mix the butter and the beef stock concentrate; brush it over the steak.
— Place the steak on a rack and cook at 70% for 2 minutes.
— Give the rack a half-turn, turn the steak over and continue cooking at 70% for 2 minutes for rare steak. Cook a little longer for less rare meat.

Braised Beef

Level of Difficulty	(utensils icon)
Preparation Time	30 min
Cost per Serving	$
Number of Servings	6
Nutritional Value	385 calories 52.5 g protein 8.5 mg iron
Food Exchanges	5 oz meat 1 vegetable exchange
Cooking Time	1 h 40 min
Standing Time	10 min
Power Level	100%, 50%
Write Your Cooking Time Here	(pencil and apple icon)

Ingredients
1.4 kg (3 lb) brisket tip, cut into large pieces
30 mL (2 tablespoons) oil
750 mL (3 cups) beef stock
1 398 mL (14 oz) can tomatoes
4 carrots, cut in strips
2 Spanish onions, quartered
1 turnip, cut in strips
4 cloves
1 mL (1/4 teaspoon) allspice
2 bayleaves
salt and pepper

Method
— Preheat a browning dish at 100% for 7 minutes.
— Add the oil and sear the meat on all sides; remove meat and set aside.
— Add the vegetables and cook at 100% for 6 minutes; stir in the beef stock, tomatoes and spices.
— Bring to a boil; cook at 100% for 6 to 8 minutes.
— Add the meat and cook at 50% for 45 minutes.
— Turn the meat over and continue cooking at 50% for 45 minutes, or until the meat is tender.
— Take out the meat and vegetables; remove the fat from the surface of the stock; strain.
— Prepare a *beurre manié* by softening some butter and adding an equal quantity of flour; stir into the sauce and keep stirring until it thickens.
— Cook at 100% until the sauce reaches the desired consistency, stirring every 2 minutes. Serve.

Assemble all the ingredients required for the recipe. Cut the meat and vegetables as instructed.

When you have cooked the vegetables for 6 minutes, stir in the beef stock, tomatoes and spices.

Strain the stock after removing excess fat.

Beef with Olives

Level of Difficulty	
Preparation Time	10 min
Cost per Serving	$ $
Number of Servings	6 to 8
Nutritional Value	6 servings: 514 calories 54.6 g protein 8.5 mg iron	8 servings: 385 calories 40.9 g protein 6.4 mg iron
Food Exchanges	6 servings: 6 oz meat 2 fat exchanges	8 servings: 5 oz meat 1 fat exchange
Cooking Time	1 h 30 min
Standing Time	10 min
Power Level	100%, 50%
Write Your Cooking Time Here	

Ingredients
1.5 kg (3-1/4 lb) beef, cubed
50 mL (1/4 cup) olive oil
1 large onion, chopped
2 cloves garlic, chopped
45 mL (3 tablespoons) flour
salt and pepper
250 mL (1 cup) red wine
250 mL (1 cup) beef stock
48 stuffed olives

Method
— Preheat a browning dish at 100% for 7 minutes.
— Dredge the meat with flour and sear it.
— Add the onion, garlic and seasoning; stir in the red wine and beef stock; cook at 100% for 3 minutes.
— Continue cooking at 100% for 5 minutes; reduce the power level to 50% and cook for 75 minutes, or until the meat is tender. Stir halfway through the cooking time.
— Allow to stand for ten minutes, add the olives and serve.

Assemble the ingredients required for this succulent dish.

Dredge the meat with flour before cooking. At the same time, preheat the browning dish.

Sear the floured meat, then add the onion, garlic, red wine, beef stock and seasoning.

Add the olives just before serving, when the cooking is complete.

Stuffed Cabbage Rolls

Level of Difficulty	🍴🍴
Preparation Time	40 min
Cost per Serving	$
Number of Servings	8
Nutritional Value	327 calories 2.7 g protein 4.9 mg iron
Food Exchanges	3 oz meat 1/2 bread exchange 2 vegetable exchanges
Cooking Time	45 min
Standing Time	None
Power Level	100%, 70%
Write Your Cooking Time Here	

Ingredients
900 g (2 lb) lean ground beef
125 mL (1/2 cup) cheddar cheese, grated
125 mL (1/2 cup) long-grain rice, uncooked
1 540 mL (19 oz) can tomato juice
1 160 mL (5-1/2 oz) can tomato paste
1 398 mL (14 oz) can Italian-style tomato sauce
1 green cabbage
salt and pepper
oregano

Method
— Remove the cabbage heart; cook the cabbage in 50 mL (1/4 cup) boiling water at 100% for 5 to 7 minutes, covered with plastic wrap; turn halfway through the cooking time.
— Mix the cheese with the ground beef.
— Remove the leaves from the cabbage and stuff them with 15 mL (1 tablespoon) rice and a scoop of ground beef; fold the leaf around the filling and secure with a toothpick.
— Combine the liquid ingredients; season.
— Arrange the stuffed cabbage leaves in a pan; pour the tomato sauce over them.

— Cook at 100% for 7 minutes; give dish a half-turn and continue cooking at 70% for 15 minutes. Rearrange the cabbage rolls, moving those in the center to the edge of the dish and continue cooking at 70% for 15 to 17 minutes. Serve.

Lovers of Italian cooking will really enjoy this delicious recipe which combines ground beef, cabbage, tomatoes and cheese.

When you have removed the cabbage heart, cook the cabbage itself in boiling water for 5 to 7 minutes, covered with plastic wrap.

Stuff each cabbage leaf with some rice and some beef and cheese mixture. Secure the roll with a toothpick.

71

Ground Beef Casserole

Level of Difficulty	
Preparation Time	15 min
Cost per Serving	$
Number of Servings	4
Nutritional Value	263 calories 28.4 g protein 5 mg iron
Food Exchanges	3 oz meat 2 vegetable exchanges
Cooking Time	16 min
Standing Time	5 min
Power Level	100%
Write Your Cooking Time Here	

Ingredients
450 g (1 lb) lean ground beef
225 g (1/2 lb) green beans,
cut into 2.5 cm (1 inch)
lengths
2 celery stalks, chopped
250 mL (1 cup) beef stock
125 g (4 oz) mushrooms,
halved
455 mL (16 oz) can of
tomatoes, drained
10 mL (2 teaspoons)
Worcestershire sauce
salt and pepper
10 mL (2 teaspoons) parsley
pinch oregano, thyme and
garlic powder

Method
— Precook the celery and
mushrooms; cook the
green beans at 100% for 5
to 6 minutes; stir halfway
through the cooking time.
— Mix the ground beef and
cook at 100% for 3
minutes, stir and continue
cooking at 100% for 3
minutes.
— Stir in the green beans,
the other ingredients and
the beef stock combined
with the liquid from the
tomatoes; cut up the
tomatoes and add them.
— Cover and cook at 100%
for 5 minutes; let stand
for 5 minutes and serve.

Arrange the green beans in a microwave-safe casserole with a lid.

Cook the ground beef separately and stir in the green beans along with all the other ingredients.

MICROTIPS

When freezing large quantities of ground beef, divide it into blocks of 450 to 700 g (1 to 1-1/2 lb) and hollow out the center of each to make defrosting easier.

To Heat Buns
Two minutes are enough to heat buns in the microwave oven. Put a dozen buns in a basket with a dinner serviette. Cover the buns with the serviette, heat at 100% for 30 seconds. Check the temperature of the buns and repeat the process until they are warm.

Beef Omelette

Level of Difficulty	
Preparation Time	30 min
Cost per Serving	$
Number of Servings	4
Nutritional Value	320 calories 26.1 g protein 4.5 mg iron
Food Exchanges	3 oz meat 1/2 bread exchange 1 vegetable exchange 1 fat exchange
Cooking Time	15 min
Standing Time	None
Power Level	100%, 70%
Write Your Cooking Time Here	

Ingredients
350 g (12 oz) lean ground beef
1 onion, chopped
15 mL (1 tablespoon) soy sauce
30 mL (2 tablespoons) butter
350 g (12 oz) potatoes, grated
5 eggs
50 mL (1/4 cup) 2% milk
2 mL (1/2 teaspoon) paprika
pepper

Method
— Cook the meat and the onion at 100% for 4 minutes; add the soy sauce.
— Melt the butter at 100% for 1 minute in a pie plate, add the potatoes and cook at 100% for 4 minutes; give the plate a half-turn halfway through the cooking time.
— Combine all the other ingredients and add to the cooked potatoes; cook at 100% for 1 minute.
— Add the cooked beef; cook at 70% for 1 minute.
— Lift up the edges of the omelette so that any uncooked egg can run underneath; continue cooking at 70% for 4 minutes, or until the omelette is cooked, turning the dish halfway through the cooking time.

Eggs, onion, grated potatoes and ground beef are the main ingredients of this easy-to-make recipe.

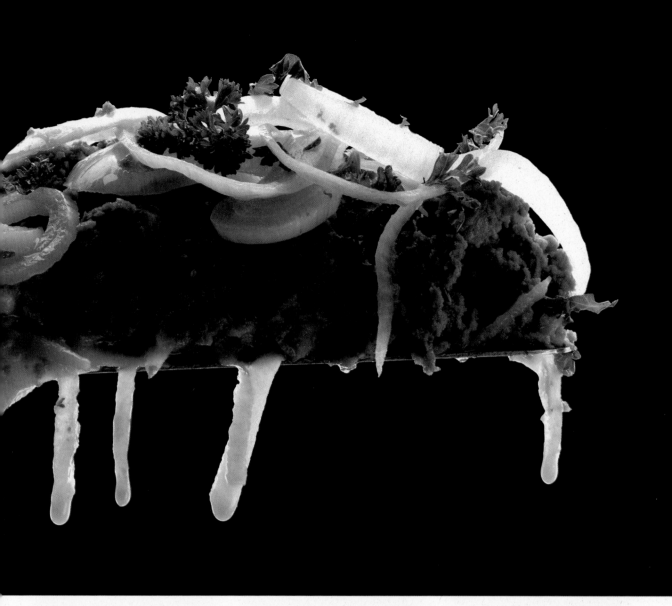

When the grated potatoes are cooked, add the mixture of soy sauce, eggs, milk, paprika and pepper.

Add the cooked meat to the mixture thus obtained and cook at 70% for 1 minute.

Spread the omelette out evenly before the last stage of cooking. Lift up the edges so that any uncooked egg can run underneath.

Beef Ramekins

Level of Difficulty	🍴
Preparation Time	20 min
Cost per Serving	$
Number of Servings	6
Nutritional Value	222 calories 18.5 g protein 2.9 mg iron
Food Exchanges	2 oz meat 1/2 bread exchange 1 vegetable exchange
Cooking Time	10 min
Standing Time	3 min
Power Level	100%, 70%
Write Your Cooking Time Here	

Ingredients
450 g (1 lb) lean ground beef
125 mL (1/2 cup) 18% cream
1 egg
125 mL (1/2 cup) rolled oats
30 mL (2 tablespoons) finely chopped celery
4 green onions, finely chopped
4 crackers, crumbled
salt and pepper
5 mL (1 teaspoon) tarragon
6 slices red pepper

Method
— Place a slice of red pepper at the bottom of each ramekin dish.
— Combine all the other ingredients and fill dishes with the mixture.
— Cook at 100% for 3 minutes; reduce the power level to 70% and continue cooking for 7 minutes, giving the dishes a half-turn halfway through the cooking time.
— Allow to stand for 3 minutes, turn out and serve with Bordelaise sauce.

Assemble the ingredients for this unpretentious and inexpensive dish.

Place a slice of red pepper at the bottom of each ramekin dish.

Fill each dish with the meat mixture.

When ramekins are cooked and the standing time is over, turn out onto plates before serving.

Hamburgers

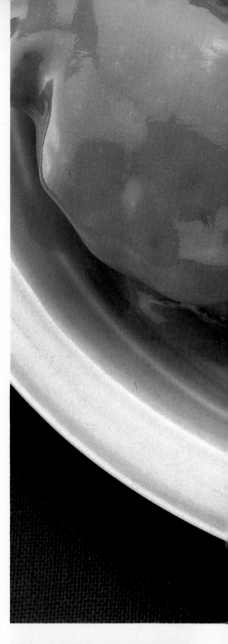

Level of Difficulty	
Preparation Time	15 min
Cost per Serving	$
Number of Servings	4
Nutritional Value	358 calories 28.9 g protein 4.3 mg iron
Food Exchanges	3-1/2 oz meat 2 vegetable exchanges 1 fat exchange
Cooking Time	12 min
Standing Time	None
Power Level	90%, 100%
Write Your Cooking Time Here	

Ingredients
450 g (1 lb) lean ground beef
1 egg
3 medium onions, cut into rings
1 medium onion, finely chopped
salt and pepper
15 mL (1 tablespoon) soy sauce
1 packet instant beef gravy, requiring 4 minutes to prepare

Method
— Mix the ground beef, egg and finely chopped onion; shape into 4 large patties.
— Arrange the patties on a bacon rack; cook at 90% for 7 to 8 minutes.
— Mix the onion rings and the soy sauce; cook at 100% for 4 minutes; stir halfway through the cooking time; arrange over the patties.
— Serve with an instant beef gravy from a mix.

Arrange the patties on a bacon rack so that the fat will drain out during cooking.

Slice onions into rings and mix with soy sauce; cook in a small bowl covered with plastic wrap.

Use a small whisk to prepare an instant beef gravy from a mix, readily available in most stores.

Before serving, arrange the onions on the cooked patties, and cover with gravy.

Meat Loaf with Spinach

Level of Difficulty	(difficulty icon)
Preparation Time	35 min
Cost per Serving	$
Number of Servings	6
Nutritional Value	364 calories 32.8 g protein 6 mg iron
Food Exchanges	4 oz meat 2 vegetable exchanges
Cooking Time	24 min
Standing Time	5 min
Power Level	100%, 70%
Write Your Cooking Time Here	

Ingredients
Stuffing
300 g (10 oz) fresh spinach
250 mL (1 cup) thinly sliced
mushrooms
125 mL (1/2 cup) chopped
onion
50 mL (1/4 cup) parsley
125 mL (1/2 cup)
breadcrumbs
1 egg
nutmeg
salt and pepper

Meat
675 g (1-1/2 lb) lean ground
beef
250 mL (1 cup) grated
cheddar cheese
125 mL (1/2 cup)
breadcrumbs
1 egg
10 mL (2 teaspoons)
Worcestershire sauce
salt and pepper

Method
Stuffing
— Wash the spinach; cook at
  100% for 5 minutes then
  drain, squeezing out
  excess liquid.
— Cook the mushrooms and
  onion at 100% for 3
  minutes; pour off the
  liquid released during
  cooking.
— Add the parsley, bread-
  crumbs, egg, nutmeg, salt
  and pepper; add the
  spinach and mix well.
Meat
— Combine the ground beef,
  cheddar cheese, bread-
  crumbs, egg, Worcester-
  shire sauce, salt and

pepper.
— Spread out on wax paper
  in a rectangle about 1 cm
  (1/2 in) thick; cover with
  an even layer of stuffing;
  roll up from the narrower
  end, jelly roll style. Use
  the paper to lift and fold
  the meat over into a tight
  roll, peeling it back as you
  go.
— Place in a dish; cook at
  100% for 8 minutes; turn
  the dish, reduce power
  level to 70% and continue
  cooking for 8 minutes.
— Allow to stand for 5
  minutes and serve.

Use a sieve and spoon to squeeze the moisture out of the spinach before making the stuffing.

These are the two types of dishes most commonly used for cooking meat loaves.

Using a rolling pin, spread the meat mixture on wax paper and roll it out till it is about 1 cm (1/2 in) thick.

Spread the stuffing over the meat and fold over jelly roll style into a fairly tight roll.

Place the meat loaf in the center of a rectangular dish and cook it. Turn the dish once during cooking.

Meat Loaves

Meat loaves are made from ground meat and can be served with literally any sauce or seasoning. You are limited only by your imagination and your personal preferences.

It is best to use lean meat, otherwise the results can be disappointing.

To test whether or not a meat loaf is done, insert a thermometer into the center. The loaf is cooked if the temperature is between 145°C and 150°C (290°-300°F). If you do not have a thermometer, stick a knife into the center of the loaf. The loaf is done if the juice that runs out is clear.

Ring dishes will help to ensure even cooking of meat loaves, and we recommend that you use them. Because there is no meat in the center of these dishes, you do not have to worry about the fact that the center would cook more slowly than the meat around the edges.

If you decide to freeze your meat loaves, do not leave them in the freezer for more than a month. To defrost them, heat at 30% for 20 to 30 minutes. Once defrosted, uncooked loaves will require the same cooking time as that given in the recipe.

Meat Loaf with Sweet and Sour Sauce

Ingredients

900 g (2 lb) lean ground beef
1 onion, chopped

250 mL (1 cup) cooked rice
250 mL (1 cup) beef stock
2 eggs, beaten

75 mL (1/3 cup) soy sauce
5 mL (1 teaspoon) parsley
1 or 2 cloves garlic, chopped
5 mL (1 teaspoon) salt
2 mL (1/2 teaspoon) pepper
340 mL (12 oz) ready-made
sweet and sour sauce, available in stores.

Level of Difficulty	🍴
Preparation Time	10 min
Cost per Serving	$
Number of Servings	6
Nutritional Value	398 calories 34.7 g protein 6.4 mg iron
Food Exchanges	4 oz meat 1/2 bread exchange 1 fat exchange
Cooking Time	23 min
Standing Time	None
Power Level	100%, 70%
Write Your Cooking Time Here	

Method

— Combine all ingredients except the sauce; shape into a loaf.
— Cook at 100% for 8 minutes; turn the dish, reduce power level to 70% and continue cooking for 7 to 9 minutes.
— Heat the ready-made sauce at 100% for 2 to 4 minutes; stir halfway through the cooking time.
— Cover the loaf with the sauce.

Meat Loaf with Chili Sauce

Level of Difficulty	
Preparation Time	15 min
Cost per Serving	**$**
Number of Servings	5
Nutritional Value	331 calories 32 g protein 5.5 mg iron
Food Exchanges	4 oz meat 1 vegetable exchange
Cooking Time	20 min
Standing Time	5 min
Power Level	100%, 70%
Write Your Cooking Time Here	

Ingredients

675 g (1-1/2 lb) lean ground beef
125 mL (1/2 cup) wheatgerm
1 large carrot, grated
125 mL (1/2 cup) finely chopped onion
125 mL (1/2 cup) milk
50 mL (1/4 cup) chili sauce
1 egg, beaten
10 mL (2 teaspoons) Worcestershire sauce
2 mL (1/2 teaspoon) Dijon mustard
salt and pepper
pinch of chili powder

Method

— Mix the milk and the eggs with the chili sauce and the Worcestershire sauce.
— In another bowl, combine all the other ingredients.
— Combine the two mixtures in a loaf pan; cook at 100% for 5 minutes.
— Turn the dish, reduce power level to 70% and continue cooking for 15 minutes.
— Top with extra chili sauce, allow to stand for 5 minutes and serve.

Assemble the ingredients required for this quick and economical meat loaf.

84

When you have combined the milk, eggs, chili sauce and Worcestershire sauce, mix the meat with the remaining ingredients.

Combine the two mixtures in a loaf pan making sure to mix thoroughly. Spread evenly and cook according to the instructions given in the recipe.

MICROTIPS

It is possible to freeze meat loaves for up to a month. To do so, allow to cool completely, wrap carefully and freeze. To defrost, heat at 30% for 20 to 30 minutes.

Meatballs

A simple basic recipe, which you can liven up with your choice of sauce

Level of Difficulty	🍴
Preparation Time	20 min
Cost per Serving	**$**
Number of Servings	about 36 meatballs
Cooking Time	3 x 8 min
Standing Time	None
Power Level	100%
Write Your Cooking Time Here	

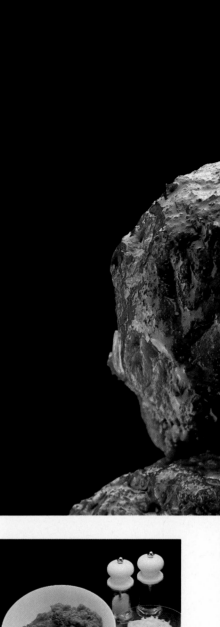

Ingredients
1.4 kg (3 lb) lean ground beef
175 mL (3/4 cup) breadcrumbs
3 onions, chopped
5 eggs, beaten
45 mL (3 tablespoons) beef stock concentrate (Bovril)
salt and pepper

Method
— Combine all the ingredients and shape into meatballs.
— Cook one-third at a time on a bacon rack at 100% for 8 minutes; turn the dish halfway through the cooking time.

Assemble all the ingredients for this basic recipe, which is inexpensive and easy to make.

When you have combined all the ingredients, shape the mixture into evenly sized meatballs.

Arrange the meatballs on a circular bacon rack, so that the fat can drain out during cooking.

Cook each batch of a dozen or so meatballs for 8 minutes, turning the rack halfway through the cooking time.

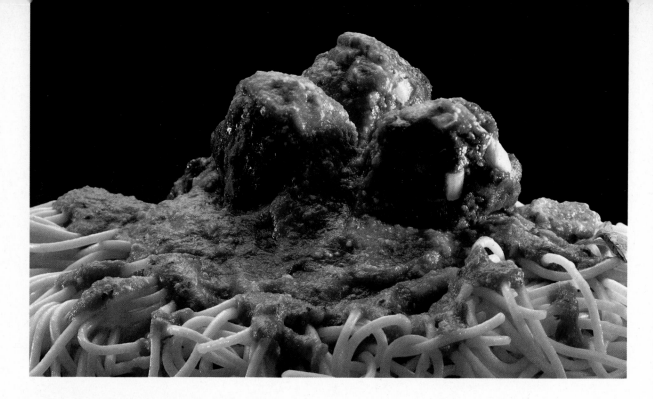

Italian Sauce
with Meatballs

Transforms a plate of pasta into an irresistible festival
of color and aromas.

Level of Difficulty	
Preparation Time	10 min
Cost per Serving	$
Number of Servings	6
Nutritional Value	433 calories 30.9 g protein 5.2 mg iron
Food Exchanges	4.5 oz meat 2 vegetable exchanges 1/2 bread exchange
Cooking Time	6 min
Standing Time	None
Power Level	100%
Write Your Cooking Time Here	

Ingredients
426 mL (15 oz) tomato sauce
2 mL (1/2 teaspoon) basil
2 mL (1/2 teaspoon) oregano
30 mL (2 tablespoons) parsley
30 mL (2 tablespoons) grated
parmesan cheese
pinch garlic salt

Method
— Combine all the
  ingredients and cook at
  100% for 3 minutes.
— Add 18 cooked meatballs
  prepared according to the
  basic recipe; cook at
  100% for 3 minutes and
  serve.

Sweet and Sour Sauce with Meatballs

A delicious sauce for any garnish or rice dish.

Level of Difficulty	🍴🍴
Preparation Time	10 min
Cost per Serving	💲
Number of Servings	6
Nutritional Value	374 calories 28.7 g protein 5 mg iron
Food Exchanges	4 oz meat 1/2 bread exchange 1/2 fruit exchange
Cooking Time	7 min
Standing Time	None
Power Level	100%
Write Your Cooking Time Here	

Ingredients
1 398 mL (14 oz) can crushed pineapple
75 mL (5 tablespoons) wine vinegar
15 mL (1 tablespoon) cornstarch
30 mL (2 tablespoons) fruit ketchup
1 green pepper, chopped
5 mL (1 teaspoon) ground ginger

Method
— Stir the cornstarch into the wine vinegar.
— Add the resulting mixture to the other ingredients; mix well.
— Cook at 100% for 2 minutes; stir, then continue cooking at 100% for 2 minutes.
— Add 18 cooked meatballs prepared according to the basic recipe; cook at 100% for 3 minutes and serve.

All-Purpose Ground Beef Base

Level of Difficulty	▮▮▮
Preparation Time	30 min
Cost per Serving	$
Number of Servings	4 x 6
Nutritional Value	86 calories 17.6 mg protein 1.5 mg iron
Cooking Time	46 min
Standing Time	None
Power Level	100%, 90%
Write Your Cooking Time Here	

Ingredients
2.25 kg (5 lb) lean ground beef
4 medium onions, chopped
3 cloves garlic, chopped
60 mL (4 tablespoons) olive oil
375 mL (12.5 oz) chili sauce
1 packet onion soup
1 packet brown gravy mix
10 mL (2 teaspoons) salt

Method
— Cook onion and garlic in oil at 100% for 3 to 5 minutes; stir once or twice during cooking.
— Add the ground beef; mix well and cook at 90% for 14 to 16 minutes, stirring 2 or 3 times during cooking.
— Add the rest of the ingredients; mix well.
— Cover and cook at 100% for 5 to 8 minutes.
— Allow to cool and freeze in 4 equal portions.

Make this dish, divide it into 4 portions and freeze to have on hand for impromptu meals.

Macaroni Stir-Fry

A fast, inexpensive dish with an exotic touch.

Ingredients
340 g (3/4 lb) macaroni
1/4 recipe ground beef base,
defrosted (see recipe page 90)
2 green peppers
4 stalks celery
2 onions
15 mL (1 tablespoon) butter
soy sauce
pepper

Method
— Cook the macaroni and
  cut up the vegetables.
— Melt butter at 100% for
  30 to 40 seconds.
— Add the vegetables; cook
  at 100% for 2 to 4
  minutes.
— Heat the meat at 70% for
  2 to 3 minutes.
— Mix the cooked meat,
  vegetables and macaroni
  together; add pepper and
  soy sauce. This dish can
  be reheated at 70% for 3
  to 5 minutes.

Level of Difficulty	🍴
Preparation Time	30 min
Cost per Serving	$
Number of Servings	6
Nutritional Value	396 calories 25.5 g protein 0.8 mg iron
Food Exchanges	3 oz meat 2 bread exchanges 1 vegetable exchange
Cooking Time	15 min
Standing Time	None
Power Level	100%, 70%
Write Your Cooking Time Here	

Shepherd's Pie

Easy to make and a real family pleaser

Ingredients

625 mL (2-1/2 cups) mashed potatoes
1/4 recipe ground beef base, defrosted (see recipe page 90)
5 mL (1 teaspoon) beef stock powder
1 420 g (14 oz) package whole kernel corn, defrosted
125 mL (1/2 cup) grated cheddar cheese (yellow)
1 egg
5 mL (1 teaspoon) parsley
1/2 mL (1/8 teaspoon) paprika

Level of Difficulty	🍴
Preparation Time	35 min
Cost per Serving	$
Number of Servings	6
Nutritional Value	380 calories 27 g protein 5.5 mg iron
Food Exchanges	4 oz meat 1 bread exchange 1 vegetable exchange
Cooking Time	15 min
Standing Time	None
Power Level	100%, 70%
Write Your Cooking Time Here	✏️

Method
— Put the defrosted ground beef base into a container.
— Mix in the beef stock powder and stir.
— Arrange the defrosted corn over the beef mixture.
— Prepare the mashed potatoes; add the egg, parsley and paprika; mix.
— Spread the mashed potatoes over the corn; cook at 100% for 5 minutes, then reduce the power level to 70% and continue cooking for 8 to 10 minutes.
— Garnish with grated cheese.

Chili

A quick and simple dish that can be served
with rice or potatoes

Level of Difficulty	
Preparation Time	10 min
Cost per Serving	$
Number of Servings	6
Nutritional Value	340 calories 25.1 g protein 5.5 mg iron
Food Exchanges	4 oz meat 1 vegetable exchange
Cooking Time	10 min
Standing Time	None
Power Level	100%
Write Your Cooking Time Here	

Ingredients
1/4 recipe ground beef base,
defrosted (see recipe page 90)
1 213 mL (7.5 oz) can tomato
sauce
1 398 mL (14 oz) can red
kidney beans
10 mL (2 teaspoons) chili
powder

Method
— Combine all the
  ingredients in a container.
— Cover and cook at 100%
  for 6 to 10 minutes.

Stuffed Peppers

Ingredients
1/4 recipe ground beef base, defrosted (see recipe page 90)
250 mL (1 cup) cooked rice
1 398 mL (14 oz) can tomato sauce
2 mL (1/2 teaspoon) basil
2 mL (1/2 teaspoon) salt
1/2 mL (1/8 teaspoon) pepper
2 large green peppers
2 large red peppers
75 mL (1/3 cup) grated cheese

Level of Difficulty	🍴
Preparation Time	25 min
Cost per Serving	$
Number of Servings	4
Nutritional Value	505 calories 34.7 g protein 6.9 mg iron
Food Exchanges	5 oz meat 1 bread exchange 1 vegetable exchange
Cooking Time	12 min
Standing Time	3 to 5 min
Power Level	100%
Write Your Cooking Time Here	✏️🍎

Method
— Cut open the peppers and remove the seeds and the membranes.
— Combine beef, rice, half the tomato sauce, basil, salt and pepper.
— Arrange the peppers in a dish and stuff them with the beef mixture.
— Pour the rest of the sauce over the peppers.
— Cover and cook at 100% for 10 to 12 minutes or until done to your liking. Turn the dish halfway through the cooking.
— Sprinkle with grated cheese; continue cooking at 100% for 1 minute.
— Allow to stand for 3 to 5 minutes without removing the cover; serve.

Beef Liver in Brown Gravy

	Single Recipe	Double Recipe
Level of Difficulty		
Preparation Time	10 min*	10 min*
Cost per Serving	$	$
Number of Servings	3	6
Nutritional Value	408 calories 31.1 g protein 10.2 mg iron	
Food Exchanges	3 oz meat 1 vegetable exchange 2 fat exchanges	
Cooking Time	10 min	12 min
Standing Time	None	None
Power Level	100%, 70%	100%, 70%
Write Your Cooking Time Here		

* The liver should soak in milk in the refrigerator for 24 hours.

Ingredients

Single Recipe		Double Recipe
450 g (1 lb)	beef liver	900 g (2 lb)
15 mL (1 tablespoon)	oil	30 mL (2 tablespoons)
1	Spanish onion(s), sliced	2
500 mL (2 cups)	brown gravy (canned or from a mix)	1 L (4 cups)

Method

— Leave the liver to soak in milk for 24 hours in the refrigerator.
— Drain carefully.
— Cook the onion at 100% for 3 minutes; put aside.
— Preheat a browning dish at 100% for 7 minutes; coat with oil and return to the microwave for 30 seconds at 100%.
— Sear the liver.
— Add the hot gravy and onion to the meat.
— Cook at 70% for 8 to 10 minutes.

96

Entertaining

Menu:
Leek Soup
Beef Tenderloin Marinated in Soy
Sauce
Rice Pilaf
Cauliflower au Gratin
Carrot Cake

Having friends or relatives in to dine should be an enjoyable experience for you as well as for your guests. Whether your invitation is prompted by a sense of duty or a genuine love of entertaining, a meal is a splendid opportunity to combine good cheer, good food and good conversation. Producing a complete meal in the microwave is simple and allows even the most anxious of hosts time to relax before their guests arrive. There are just two things you must remember: choose the dishes carefully and be systematic in your preparations.

Here are some basic rules to help you work out your menus.

1. Do not include two red meats, or two white meats, prepared in different ways on the same menu.

2. Do not serve the same meat in two different ways.

3. Avoid including poultry and game birds in the same meal.

4. Do not serve dishes with similar garnishes or with sauces of the same type (such as mayonnaise and tartare sauce).

If you keep these basic principles in mind, you can give your personal tastes and even your fancies full rein. After all, cooking provides the perfect opportunity to surprise and charm your friends with your skill and inventiveness.

From the Recipe to Your Table

Order of preparation:
5 hours before the meal:
— Prepare the marinade and marinate the tenderloin.
— Prepare the cake and icing.

3 hours before the meal:
— Prepare the leek soup.

90 minutes before the meal:
— Cook the rice pilaf.

1 hour before the meal:
— Cook the cauliflower and prepare the white sauce.

50 minutes before the meal:
— Cook the tenderloin and cover with aluminum foil.

15 minutes before the meal:
— Prepare the sauce.

10 minutes before the meal:
— Reheat the soup.

5 minutes before the meal:
— Reheat the vegetables and the rice.

Leek Soup

Cooking Time:
15 to 20 minutes

Ingredients
3 leeks
1 onion
50 mL (1/4 cup) water
250 mL (1 cup) mashed
potatoes
500 to 750 mL (2 to 3 cups)
milk
salt and pepper

Method
— Cut the leeks and onion
  into strips.
— Add water, cover and
  cook at 100% for 6 to 7
  minutes.
— Allow to stand for 2 to 3
  minutes, then puree in a
  blender, adding a little
  water if necessary.
— Stir in the mashed
  potatoes and beat well to
  a consistent thickness.
— **Add milk and seasoning.**
— Cook at 70% for about 10
  minutes, without letting it
  come to a boil.

Rice Pilaf

Your choice of two or three vegetables will provide a worthy garnish for the beef tenderloin. We suggest that, whenever possible, you pick vegetables that are in season. If you are preparing this menu in winter, moderate servings of potatoes, whole young carrots and broccoli will provide an attractive variety of colors and flavors, complementing the Cauliflower au Gratin.

Ingredients
500 mL (2 cups) rice
60 mL (4 tablespoons) butter
75 mL (1/3 cup) diced celery
75 mL (1/3 cup) sliced green onions
1 L (4 cups) boiling water
4 chicken stock cubes
60 mL (4 tablespoons) soy sauce
150 mL (2/3 cup) sliced mushrooms

Method
— Melt the butter in a casserole and add the rice; cook at 100% for 3 to 4 minutes.
— Dissolve chicken stock cubes in the boiling water and stir into the rice with the celery, green onions and soy sauce; mix well.
— Cover and cook at 100% for 8 minutes; reduce power level to 70% and continue cooking for 15 minutes.
— Add the mushrooms and stir with a fork.
— Cover and allow to stand for 10 minutes.

Beef Tenderloin Marinated in Soy Sauce

Ingredients
1.5 kg (3 lb) beef tenderloin
pepper

Marinade:
75 mL (5 tablespoons) soy
sauce
2 cloves garlic, chopped
45 mL (3 tablespoons) dry
sherry
45 mL (3 tablespoons) olive
oil

Sauce:
30 mL (2 tablespoons) cognac
30 mL (2 tablespoons) water
30 mL (2 tablespoons)
cornstarch
500 mL (2 cups) tea
250 mL (1 cup) thinly sliced
mushrooms

Level of Difficulty	🍴🍴
Preparation Time	15 min*
Cost per Serving	$ $ $
Number of Servings	8
Nutritional Value	370 calories 39.3 g protein 6.45 mg iron
Food Exchanges	4 oz meat 1 vegetable exchange 1 fat exchange
Cooking Time	14 to 20 min/kg (6 to 9 min/lb)
Standing Time	10 min
Power Level	70%, 100%

Write Your Cooking Time Here

* The meat should be marinated for at least 4 hours.

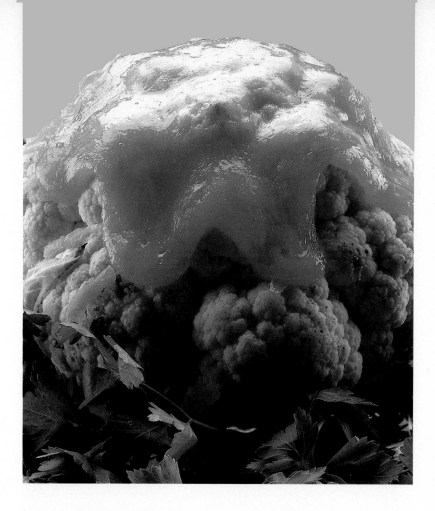

Method
— Combine the marinade
  ingredients; season the
  beef tenderloin with
  pepper and tie it; leave it
  to marinate for at least 4
  hours at room tempera-
  ture; turn and spoon some
  of the marinade over it
  every hour.
— Drain the beef carefully;
  pour the remaining
  marinade into a cooking
  dish.
— Cook the meat on a rack
  till done to your liking.
— Remove the string and
  garnish with green onions,
  lemon or parsley.
— Deglaze the pan, add the
  cognac, tea and the
  cornstarch mixed with
  water; cook at 100% for 4
  minutes, stirring halfway
  through the cooking time.
— Add the mushrooms and
  serve.

Cauliflower au Gratin

Ingredients
1 whole cauliflower
7 mL (1-1/2 teaspoons) sugar
15 mL (1 tablespoon) butter
30 mL (2 tablespoons) grated
cheese
30 mL (2 tablespoons)
breadcrumbs
1 green onion, chopped
salt and pepper

Method
— Wash the cauliflower and
  remove the leaves.
— Sprinkle the sugar over
  the bottom of a casserole,
  then put in the head.
— Cook the cauliflower at
  100% for 6 minutes or
  more, turning the dish
  halfway through the
  cooking time.
— Add the butter, green
  onion, salt and pepper.
— Cook at 100% for 2
  minutes.
— Sprinkle the cheese and
  breadcrumbs over the
  cauliflower and cook for 1
  minute at 100%.

Carrot Cake

Ingredients

500 mL (2 cups) sugar
500 mL (2 cups) flour
7 mL (1-1/2 teaspoons)
baking soda
10 mL (2 teaspoons) baking
powder
10 mL (2 teaspoons)
cinnamon
10 mL (2 teaspoons) salt
250 mL (1 cup) crushed,
drained pineapple
500 mL (2 cups) grated
carrots
4 eggs
125 mL (1/2 cup) oil
250 mL (1 cup) chopped nuts
250 mL (1 cup) raisins

Method

— Sift the flour, soda,
baking powder, cinnamon
and salt and add the
sugar.
— Mix together the carrots,
pineapple, nuts, eggs, oil
and raisins.
— Combine the two
mixtures.
— Grease a 3.3 L tube pan
with "Pam."
— Pour in cake batter and
cook raised at 70% for 16
to 18 minutes, turning the
pan halfway through the
cooking time.
— Increase the power level to
100% and continue
cooking for 3 to 4
minutes.
— Allow to cool for 20 to 30
minutes and turn out onto
a serving plate.
— Frost with your favorite
icing.

MICROTIPS

To Test If Cakes Are Cooked

A cake is cooked if a
toothpick inserted
between the center and
the edge of the dish
comes out clean, or if
pressing the cake lightly
leaves no mark. Also, a
properly cooked cake
shrinks away from the
side of the pan.

Beef Terminology

Over the course of its history, cooking, like all the great arts, has developed its own specialized terminology. The terms may refer to techniques or to characteristics of foods or dishes. As you will come across many of them frequently in this volume on beef, we thought it would be useful to list the more common ones.

Aromatic: Plant, leaf or herb with a strong and distinctive aroma, used to add a pleasant, subtle taste to dishes.

Ex.: saffron, chervil, tarragon, bay leaf, thyme.

Bard: To arrange thin slices of fat bacon on the bottom or sides of a cooking dish to protect meat during cooking and to supply extra fat. (Do not confuse with larding.)

Baste: To pour over meat that is cooking the juice and melted fat that seeps out of it.

Beurre manié: Butter softened till it is quite malleable and then mixed with an equal amount of flour.

Bouquet garni: Herbs and aromatics tied between two small sticks of celery or sprigs of parsley, used for flavoring certain dishes (soups, stews, etc.).

Braise: To cook slowly in a little liquid over a gentle heat in a covered dish in order to keep all the juices in the meat.

Deglaze: To pour a liquid such as water, a good dry wine, cream or vinegar into the container that has been used for cooking meat in order to make use of the juices that have seeped out in the course of cooking.

Dredge: See flour.

Flambe: To pour spirits over meat and set aflame.

Flour: To cover the surface of meat lightly and evenly with flour.

Fricassee: Meat cut into pieces, stewed and served with a thick gravy.

Garnish: To enhance the appearance of a dish after it is cooked by adding something, usually another food.

Glaze:	To brush a mixture over the surface of meat to give it a glossy appearance and/or add flavor.
Lard:	To insert strips of fat bacon into meat to supply extra fat during cooking.
Marbled:	Meat that contains fine lines of fat running through it. Good quality meat is usually lightly marbled.
Marinate:	To steep in a liquid so that the foodstuff takes on the flavor of the liquid; particularly used to refer to steeping meat in a marinade (a mixture of oil, lemon juice, wine or vinegar) to tenderize as well as flavor it.
Reduce:	To boil a mixture to evaporate surplus liquid to enhance the flavor and produce a thicker texture.
Scald:	To heat a liquid to just below boiling point.
Sear:	To give meat an initial cooking over a very high heat.
Season:	To add salt, pepper, spices to food in order to enhance flavor.
Simmer:	To cook over a gentle heat at just below boiling point.
Tenderize:	To soften meats by marinating them, pounding them with a mallet or piercing them all over.
Whip:	To beat air into a substance using a hand or electric egg whisk to make it light and thick.

Culinary Terms

Have you ever been faced
with a menu and found
yourself unable to understand
the terms used to describe
certain dishes? Of the many
culinary terms that exist, the
majority are French in origin.
To help you find your way
about, here is a short list of
terms and their meanings:

Bordelaise: with marrow from a meat bone
as a main ingredient.

Bourguignonne: with pieces of fat bacon,
mushrooms and small onions as main
ingredients.

Crecy: with carrots as a main ingredient.

Diable (à la): with vinegar and mustard as
main ingredients.

Espagnole: with tomatoes, onions and
peppers as main ingredients.

Forestière: with mushrooms as a main
ingredient.

Lyonnaise: with onions as a main
ingredient.

Parmentier: with potatoes as a main
ingredient.

Provençale: with tomatoes and garlic as
main ingredients.

Soubise: with onions as a main ingredient.

Washington: with corn as a main ingredient.

Conversion Chart

**Conversion Chart for the
Main Measures Used in
Cooking**

Volume
1 teaspoon. . . . . 5 mL
1 tablespoon. . . . . 15 mL

1 quart (4 cups). . . . . . 1 litre
1 pint (2 cups). . . . . . 500 mL
1/2 cup. . . . . 125 mL
1/4 cup. . . . . 50 mL

Weight
2.2 lb. . . . . 1 kg (1000 g)
1.1 lb. . . . . 500 g
0.5 lb. . . . . 225 g
0.25 lb. . . . . 115 g

1 oz. . . . . 30 g

**Metric Equivalents
for Cooking
Temperatures**

49°C. . . . . 120°F	120°C. . . . . 250°F
54°C. . . . . 130°F	135°C. . . . . 275°F
60°C. . . . . 140°F	150°C. . . . . 300°F
66°C. . . . . 150°F	160°C. . . . . 325°F
71°C. . . . . 160°F	180°C. . . . . 350°F
77°C. . . . . 170°F	190°C. . . . . 375°F
82°C. . . . . 180°F	200°C. . . . . 400°F
93°C. . . . . 200°F	220°C. . . . . 425°F
107°C. . . . . 225°F	230°C. . . . . 450°F

Readers will note that, in the recipes, we give 250 mL as the
equivalent for 1 cup and 450 g as the equivalent for 1 lb and
that fractions of these measurements are even less
mathematically accurate. The reason for this is that
mathematically accurate conversions are just not practical in
cooking. Your kitchen scales are simply not accurate enough
to weigh 454 g—the true equivalent of 1 lb—and it would be
a waste of time to try. The conversions given in this series,
therefore, necessarily represent approximate equivalents, but
they will still give excellent results in the kitchen. No problems
should be encountered if you adhere to either metric or
imperial measurements throughout a recipe.

Index